MW01059264

Angler Management

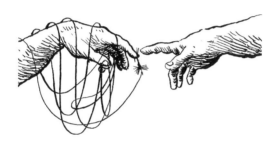

ANGLER
MANAGEMENT
THE DAY I DIED WHILE FLY FISHING
& OTHER STORIES

JACK OHMAN

HEADWATER
BOOKS

To
Ace, Mrs. Mutt,
and Fuzzy—the Danger
Loons. To the LS. To Dad and
my brother Jim, as well as Jo and
Michael. To Kevin Kallaugher, a fly-
fishing cartoonist who does both way
better than I do. And to all my fishing
friends, thank you for letting me
write down all the things you
said and do.

© 2009 by Headwater Books

Published by

HEADWATER BOOKS
531 Harding Street
New Cumberland, PA 17070
www.headwaterbooks.com

All illustrations by the author
Book design by Ryan Scheife, Mayfly Design

Printed in United States of America

First edition

10 9 8 7 6 5 4 3 2 1

ISBN: 978-1-934753-04-0

Library of Congress Control Number: 2009923106

CONTENTS

ACKNOWLEDGMENTS

Thanks to Jay Nichols of Headwater Books for encouraging me to get back in the fishing book business—and to think about doing something else. I would also like to tip a cap to the designer, Ryan Scheife, who produced a book that looks better than it actually may be. I would like to thank John Randolph and Ross Purnell of *Fly Fisherman* magazine for consistent support of my efforts. I was inspired by many people to write a book of essays and John Gierach and Ted Leeson were first among them. Finally, this book could not have been realized without a wonderful group of fellow anglers: Jim Ramsey, Dick Thomas, Steve Carter, Dave Reinhard, Allan Burdick, Rich McIntyre, and others who are in the water with me all the time and not enough.

INTRODUCTION

After I finished *An Inconvenient Trout,* which I recommend highly for its technical information and helpful how-to hints, such as not drowning, I decided almost immediately that I had more to say about fly fishing. So I really pretty much just kept on writing for another nine months, and not just because I have two kids in college and a third within casting distance. None of them fly fish—they prefer other sporting events such as soccer, lacrosse, basketball, video games, and trying to make me see if I can survive on $1.24 in checking.

To me, fly fishing is not just a sport, it is a lifestyle choice. I fly fish, and everything else seems to radiate out from that concept. I can tell you that all other fly fishermen are like that as well; everything we do is an afterthought compared with fly fishing. Jobs are performed so fly fishing can be supported, relationships are arranged around major hatches, and vehicles are purchased not only to get from Point A to Point B, but they must have the ability to go to fly fishing. Everything. Everything is plotted around fly fishing.

Including emotions.

I have experienced the full range of human emotions while fly fishing: love, hate, ambivalence, denial, empathy, fear, and, most important, anger. Why anger? Besides the fact that I am a male who, like all males, kind of enjoys a healthy dose of anger once in awhile, anger can help you with your fly fishing. The question is, does it take over your life, like a particularly nasty leader tangle or the discovery of your best friend standing in your drift, smiling defensively and cheesily, knowing full well that you are about to immerse him in the river, and not to save his soul. In order to assuage these many moments of fly-fishing anger, we must turn to humor. Comedy is easy, fly fishing is hard.

Writing about the funny things that happen in fly fishing isn't hard. It just depends on what some other angler thinks is funny. For example, bowling is, as a concept, intrinsically more amusing than fly fishing, and yet, I have yet to sit down and write that definitive bowling humor book. I don't know, maybe it's out there, maybe it isn't, but I suspect that once you get past the gutter and PBR jokes, you won't have much of a book. The humor in fly fishing, like most other subjects, is in the small stuff. I mean, what outsider could see that a hook eyelet inadvertently covered in tippet-defying clear head cement is amusing in and of itself? When I ask non-fly fishermen to look at this stuff I have written, I get mind-numbing stares.

"You want me to read your humor book about . . . fly fishing? What's funny about fly fishing?"

"Well, you see, the knots are funny, and how they keep breaking, or just showing up by accident, and . . . you know. It's funny."

To non-fly fishermen, fly fishing is something that old guys in stinky clothes and weird hats do. Old guys in stinky clothes are kind of funny, and if you throw in weird hats, well, you've got a book my friend. And, believe me, it's been done.

A lot of fly-fishing humor is kind of unintentional. Most fly-fishing writing is decidedly unironic in the extreme. Most pieces I

have read over the years revolve around the larger life lessons that fly fishing provides, none of which I have really bothered to personally explore in writing because that's not what I do. I mean, I suppose I could bang out some pieces about how losing a big trout after hours of effort is a meta-theme for the futility of life, and I would still probably manage to make little snide remarks throughout about how the head unraveled on the fly, or that the stinky old guy fell in the river. Life lesson ruined; serious fiction loses. Humor wins.

There is a lot of physical humor in fly fishing. I have lived it. Someone falling in the water is funny, no matter how gracefully he does it. Fly casting is a massive sight gag each time we attempt to do it. It almost makes no sense that it would work in the first place, and the utter stupidity with which a trout sometimes takes a ridiculous-looking wad of fur and feathers almost always strikes me as unintentionally funny.

I have often thought that what fly-fishing humor really needs are amusing fly-fishing gag items, like a fly reel with a joy buzzer attached, or mayfly-flavored gum, or a zinger that shoots a little stream of water into an unsuspecting victim's eye when he looks at it. The thing is, all fly-fishing gear, when used incorrectly, becomes gag items. The reels that have Gag Exploding Spools, the Amazing Gag Breaking Tippet Material in Key Situations, and the Gag Fly with No Hook Point That You've Been Casting for 25 Minutes are all common angling humor experiences.

Consider the broken-hook-point fly. This happens to me all the time. Gee, why did I miss that strike? Golly, I won't bother to check my fly, that's simply too much trouble. I will continue to fruitlessly cast until I give up on the pattern. Then the hatch is over.

Then I decide a new rod and reel will help.

Yet another great moment in fly-fishing humor.

THE CONVERSATION

If I really want to get rid of someone, I bring up fly fishing in conversation.

Excepting golf, a conversation about fly fishing can, to the uninitiated, work way better at encouraging profound rapid eye movement than Lunesta with a beer back. I have fended off more unwanted conversational partners by bringing up fly fishing than any other personally odious habits I can conjure up. That's not to say that I don't enjoy a wide-ranging conversation about hook points—I do. It's just that others don't.

Except if you're one of Us.

Non-fly fishermen tend to ask a lot of obvious questions about fly fishing. They ask you if you actually use live houseflies, or whether you "fly ties," or why fly fishing is morally and ethically superior to other types of fishing (it is, kind of). They will ask, "Why do you throw them back if you want to catch them, anyway?" and "How come you need all that stuff?" Believe me, we have way less stuff than the average bass-boat owner. I used to own a bass boat—I know. A bass boat alone requires the ability to do on-the-spot large-engine repair (I felt like a NASCAR pit crew), a constant monitoring of an aerated livewell (worse than trying to keep tropical fish alive), the monitoring of more sophisticated electronics than the USS *Nimitz* ("is that a carp flash, a bass flash, or a Russian submarine?"), and—because of submerged stumps and obstructions—the eternal vigilance of a NORAD missile silo launch officer.

"Sir, authenticate incoming message regarding bass target."

"Message authenticated . . . it's a 3-pound largemouth."

"Yes, sir."

In short, a pain in the ass.

And don't get me started on my old tackle box: 32 different types of Rapalas, plastic worms in a spectrum of colors ranging from infrared to ultraviolet (which worked only in teenagers' bedrooms), snelled hooks, worm inflators, bobbers, sinkers, swivels, leaders, monofilament, hook sharpeners, PowerBait, pork rinds, Flatfish, Bass-Orenos, Lazy Ikes, Industrious Ikes, Mepps, Daredevils, Jitterbugs, Creek Chubs, Hula Poppers, Skitterbuzzes, knives, gaffs, cotter pins, scales, hook disgorgers, Jaws of Life, chainsaws, backhoes, grapple skidders, piledrivers, dental drills, and a small-theater nuclear weapon for muskies.

Muskies are very dangerous.

In contrast, fly fishing has a rod, a reel, a line, waders, a vest, and some flies. Okay, maybe I understate a bit, but it is still a relatively low-gear operation compared with the Normandy Invasion logistics required to go bass fishing.

Once we have dispatched with conversation with the outsiders, having a conversation with another fly fisherman can be either on the level of one thoracic surgeon talking to another thoracic surgeon about how to resect a pesky aorta, or as gestural as a married couple exchanging the odd glance or nod. I prefer the really arcane conversation myself; it flushes out the pretenders early in the process, like the Iowa caucuses.

For example, you may run into someone who professes to be a fly fisherman at a party. I have been introduced as a fly fisherman as my primary means of getting by in life more than once (not true, but hey . . .) and someone will volunteer that he, too, is in the brotherhood.

Then you start talking to him.

I have had a similar experience with someone who asserts, falsely, that he's "fluent" in Spanish. Then you ask him a question with the word "screwdriver" in it (*destornillador,* thank you) and it all falls apart. Then he says *un poco,* or something similar, and you know that he all of a sudden is not, in fact, fluent, and that he can barely read a menu at a Mexican restaurant. Same thing with self-described fly fishermen, in many cases.

"Jack, I am a fly fisherman."

"Cool!" I will blurt out, and launch into some speed rap about tying my own Maxima leaders, and he will stand in stunned silence as if I started asking him for the screwdriver (*destornillador*) in Spanish. Or maybe I will gently inquire as to how many rods he owns. (He usually says "one," the answer of someone who doesn't fly fish. Six is the standard respectable figure.) Or perhaps I will start yammering about the drag coefficient of a CFO IV or something, and I get this kind of blank, helpless stare that says: *Please stop. Please. I give up. I am lying. I am a poseur. I am not a true fly fisherman.*

Sometimes I will feel sorry for him and say something like, "Excellent! So . . . you have a Pflueger Medalist? What a great old classic!" and this palpable sense of defeat will spread across his face, and he will float to the surface like a squawfish after 30 seconds of barely perceptible struggle. Not that these conversations

should really result in a victory, but you just need to know how high to ratchet up the arcane conversation—the more obscure the better.

My friend Jim is a master of figuring out within, say, 90 seconds whether you know what the hell you're talking about. Maybe less. He usually sets the hook after about 30 seconds. "So . . ." (long pause) "did you see that piece in *Fly Fisherman* about the new ant body material innovation?"

And you haven't. Or, really, you meant to look at that ant body material innovation article, but you just haven't quite gotten around to it, like making that new overhead storage rack for your garage, or changing all the handles on your kitchen cabinets to match the new stove. You're gonna do it, of course. Of course.

Let's say, for fun, that you actually *did* read the ant body material innovation article. Jim will then probe you about how much of it you really retained.

"Yeah . . . did you see how this guy figured out how the polymers created all those separate air pockets that not only created buoyancy, but also created a more realistic ant body sheen when viewed through the meniscus?"

"Oh . . . yes. Yes. The meniscus sheen. Yep. I'm . . . on it."

And not only that, he knows damned well that you are totally winging it at this point, and he still doesn't let up.

"Yeah, but did you see the last three paragraphs of the article . . . about . . . *segmentation?*"

"GodDAMNIT! Fine! I didn't read the article!"

I once had lunch with John Gierach, the brilliant fly-fishing writer and author of *Trout Bum*. He started The Conversation almost immediately.

"I really like the way the wings are cocked on the X fly pattern (I couldn't remember . . . I went into I Am Out of My League Shock)."

And I was like, yeah, John, uh-huh. Fixed grin. Staring glassy-eyed. I had the facial expression of a quarterback looking for a receiver 55 yards downfield, and hoping for a tailwind. Fear. Cleveland's 240-pound defenders all over the backfield chasing my 5-foot 11-inch 180-pound skinny ass all behind the line of scrimmage. Thirteen seconds left, 4th and 19, frozen tundra of Lambeau Field, and I'm hearing the voice-over: "The executive producer of ABC Sports is Roone Arledge . . ."

Game over.

Sometimes fly-fishing conversation will not stray that far into the Fly Tying Zone, but will be more about your experiences, which any self-respecting fisherman, bait or otherwise, can chime right in on.

"Yeah, geez . . . we were on the Deschutes last spring, and the stonefly hatch was on, and a bull trout nailed an 11-incher I was reeling in (credible). And then I hooked 13 fish in 45 minutes (maybe credible), and then I had really great sex with my girlfriend when I got home (maybe, maybe not), and believe it or not, she loves that I fly fish (absolute bald-faced lie)."

Sometimes the conversation will settle into some sort of riff between you and a friend about some ancient trip you took during the Carter Administration, and you can almost *not* talk in any sort of meaningful linguistic way—maybe you just exchange memes and phonemes:

"Do you remember in 1990 when we went by that rock? Maybe it was 2003. Or 1988."

"The big rock?"

"No. The other one."

"Yeah, and they were . . ."

"Yeah. On a #24 olive midge."

"Yeah."

"Yeah. It was . . . cloudy."

"Yes. Yes it was."

"They were like ALL over the pool."

"The small pool."

"Yeah. By the log."

"The one log?"

"No. The other log."

"Oh, yeah. Sorry."

"Dumbass."

The trouble with any conversation involving fly fishing with a fellow angler is how to end it. Any anecdote that you can come up with, a really good fly fisherman has absolutely no problem whatsoever in topping. Just when you think that you've finally terminated the 45-minute chat about the relative deficiencies and merits of rubber-headed versus metal-headed hackle pliers, the Opposing Chat Buddy can come up with yet another strong argument in favor of his side. And talking about difficult casts you've made is even worse. Every single fly fisherman in America has *that one cast* that saved the day, or the trip.

"Well, it was just after a thunderstorm runoff, I was hammered on whiskey sours, a 19-inch brown was working in some bullrushes and a barbed-wire fence line across three back eddies, and I made a 70-foot cast in 45-mile-an-hour winds and put this soaked, rusty Renegade with the hackle unraveled right in front of him, and the SOB *just nailed it . . .*"

At that point, any further conversation is futile. Like fly fishing.

THE MADNESS

When I was a young boy growing up the early 1960s, a time that now seems as antiquated as the Civil War to me (our family owned a 1959 Plymouth with fins as large as a great white shark, and we drove it absolutely unironically), gas was 25 cents a gallon, America was sending these garbage cans up into space containing humans who actually volunteered to ride in them, most families I knew had black-and-white televisions, and computers were the flashing-light things I saw on *Star Trek*.

Oddly, fly fishing was part of that time for me: a mystery of the modern age that must be solved. The truth is, I was not raised in a fly-fishing environment. I was raised in a Rapala and spinning-rod environment, where fishing was merely a hobby, not a way of life, and certainly not an obsession.

Or madness.

MADNESS. Insert maniacal cackle here.

You know. Craziness, obsession, absolutely dead-nutty gaga-like-you-were-over-some-girl-in-the-fourth-grade-cuckoo fixated. On fly fishing.

Deconstructed (and you should never deconstruct something or someone you love—it leads to trouble), fly fishing seems like an unlikely object of obsession/madness. You just put a fuzzy sharp thing on a piece of string at the end of a long thing to catch a slimy thing out of wet stuff that you then do not keep. What's so compelling about that? It certainly would be explicable to be obsessed with food, sex, or something along those lines. There is a long history of pleasant feelings and experiences associated with those hobbies, not to mention the fact that they are necessary for human survival. Fly fishing, sadly, is not necessary for human survival.

Like all madness, it comes on slowly. Friends notice little changes in your personality. What once was a simple pastime becomes a reason for living, a central organizing principle, a *raison d'etre,* a metaphor, a *need.*

A kind of *disorder.*

When you first start fly fishing, you start off with one rod, one reel, one line, one vest, some flies, and a pair of waders. All of that is certainly justifiable. You need all that. But then the madness sets in. Suddenly you realize that one rod, one reel, one line, one vest, some flies, and a pair of waders is simply not enough.

You start hanging around the fly shop more. You only hang around with people (fellow madmen) who are interested in fly fishing, and only fly fishing. Soon that's all you really want to talk about. All other conversation becomes drivel. Talk of your job, relationships, possessions, goals, hopes, dreams, and ambitions goes out the window in favor of talk about fly fishing. The conversation about fly fishing is performed by wind-talkers, horse whisperers, and cryptographers whose only true language is trout and the pursuit of same. You discuss what you really need, what you really want, and how to get it. How do I get the second new rod and somehow justify it? Madness says, screw justification—you just get the second rod. Black budget it. Bury it in the Christmas tree appropriations bill. Whatever it takes . . . just get the second rod.

And you do. What about a third rod? A fourth? A 9-weight. A 2-weight. A Spey rod. A 5-piece 8'6" for a 5. A 7'9" for a 4. Any sane person knows that a 9' for a 6-weight will get you through the vast majority of situations . . . everyone but a madman, that is. The madman is now on the road to acquiring 13 rods of varying lengths, and, hey, try and stop him.

And this is just the beginning.

Size 22 midges. Lots of them. In color-coded boxes.

Driving four hours one way to hit a hatch for two hours, turning around, driving back in a thunderstorm or two. Absolutely no second thought given.

Take building your own rod—BUILDING YOUR OWN ROD? I mean, that's like telling people you're restoring a 1936 Hudson Terraplane, and it's gonna be *all* original parts. Do you know how hard it is to build your own rod? It's almost impossible. I tried it once. I would rather try prostate surgery on myself than try to build a rod again. You have to do the guide wraps so that they're perfectly even. Mine looked like they were wrapped by a guy whose hobby is collecting a large twine ball in his back yard. The varnish has to be perfectly even—you need to buy a rod turner. Do you know how insane it sounds to say you just bought a rod turner? Even the oddest step-retracing, check-the-gas, make-sure-the-locks-are-locked (again), wash-your-hands-57-times-a-day OCD fly-fishing *junkies* don't build their own fly rods. They just don't.

For the love of God, just take a look at fly-fishing magazines. They have 2,000-word articles in them about a certain type of duck feather. It's not *U.S. News & World Report*, people. They have

huge color illustrations on how to wrap lead around a small piece of piano wire. They devote pages and pages to how many cubic feet per second a river carries. Essays about orange versus red fuzz. Madness.

And then there's the weather. Weather that you wouldn't rise from bed in order to get the morning paper because it's too cold and wet (58 degrees and a light mist) is nothing compared with the kind of weather you would think nothing of to catch a few 9-inch hatchery rainbows. I once fished in a snowfall so hard that not only did my line freeze in the guides (that's nothing), but I wasn't really sure if I could find my way back to the bank without GPS and 50,000-watt klieg lights. And I was happy. I felt like Jon Krakauer, freezing to death at 23,000 feet in a small nylon tent, stepping over dead frozen sherpas in order to catch trout the size of a canned herring. Freezing rain. Nuclear blast–speed wind. Icy pellets smashing into my face like 12-ought buckshot. Nothing. I felt nothing, really, nothing but *happiness* because I had turned the corner from sanity into the psychological state known as fly fishing.

When I was in college in Minnesota, we used to have a rule: no skiing if it was below zero. In fly fishing, we don't stop fishing until the water ceases molecular motion, the fly bouncing off the ice, helpless, useless, hoping the trout had a part-time job as a U.S. Coast Guard cutter.

Heat? We don't stop fishing if mosquitoes the size of B-17s have drained every drop of blood from our brains in 102-degree heat. We don't stop fishing if our skin is burned down to the dermis and smells like a rare New York strip steak. We just put on the A1 sauce and keep casting. We don't stop fishing if the sun looks like it's about to crash onto the earth's surface. We don't stop fishing until the river turns into water vapor and doesn't flow anymore, but drifts off up in the atmosphere. We don't stop fishing even if the water has turned into magma with a hatch. We don't stop fishing if Satan comes over and asks us what pattern we're using. We. Don't. Stop. Fishing.

Period.

There must be some sort of intervention at some point. Your family and friends invite you into the living room you haven't sat in since Reagan was in the movies; they all gather around you with wide, liquid eyes (liquid! You can fish in liquid!) and tell you they love you and that you need help. Special help. Help with your, you know, Jack . . . fishing.

"Great! I need some help with my fishing! Can you tie me up some size 24 Trico spinners fast? I need to drive to Montana tonight in my diaper wearing a T-shirt that says "The Way to a Man's Heart is through His Fly."

I once actually saw a friend wearing this exact shirt on a day when then-governor Bill Clinton happened to be visiting my newspaper. The governor said, without a trace of self-knowledge, that he liked my friend's shirt.

We should have recognized a fellow fly-fishing madman when we saw one. We could have saved Ken Starr a lot of time and money.

There was a great scene in the movie *All the President's Men*. Deep Throat was relating a tale about the famously mad Watergate burglar G. Gordon Liddy.

"I was once at a party where Liddy put his hand in the flame of a candle until it burned. Someone asked, 'What's the trick?' Liddy said, 'The trick is in not minding.'"

It was then that I knew G. Gordon Liddy was a fly fisherman.

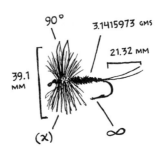

90° 3.1415973 GMS

21.32 MM

39.1 MM

(X) ∞

SCIENTIFIC ANGLERS

Liberal arts majors such as myself (History, BA, 1999, Honors Program, Barely Finished before Age 40) tend to be fly fishermen rather than bait or lure guys. This is not to suggest that we own the whole fly-fishing world, or that there isn't any cross-pollination, but most fly fishermen I know seem to be more on the English Lit/American Studies/Philosophy/History side of the equation as opposed to the sciences. And, being liberal arts majors, we tend to want to make the world line up in a humanistic way rather than a purely empirical and scientific one.

Except when it comes to fly fishing.

Ask most liberal arts people if they feel like they're a bit under-accomplished in the sciences, or even in linear thought, and most of them would agree that, yes, they are a little sheepish about their educational background. I was raised by a PhD research scientist, and I can tell you firsthand that he viewed liberal arts majors as ethereal slacker stoners with no real understanding of how the world works, let alone how to turn on a Bunsen burner or create penicillin in a petri dish (when I was a child, my dad once gave me some penicillin that he personally created—I can't even make a

Manhattan without consulting the Internet). One way that we've figured out a way to make ourselves feel, well, more *scientific*, is to inject science into art—specifically, the art of fly fishing.

I'm not really sure precisely when all this science stuff got injected into fly fishing. Fly fishing books that I read as a young teenager, such as *Trout* by Ray Bergman or *How to Fish from Top to Bottom* by Sid Gordon, were very much on the descriptive and literary end of the fly-fishing spectrum. If you're over 50 or so, most of the fly patterns we grew up with almost sounded like the titles of books we had to read in high-school English class: Red Ibis, White Miller, Green Drake.

"Jack, could you read us a passage from *The Red Ibis,* by Nathaniel Hawthorne?"

"I forgot the book, Miss Pontius."

And the rods . . . fly rods were made of bamboo until the 1940s, and then they came up with fiberglass. There were no graphite rods, just your grandfather's old cane rod in a leather case, or the Shakespeare (oops, liberal arts reference) fiberglass rod your dad bought during the Eisenhower/Pave Over Everything/Big Fin/50-Megaton/ Loud Hi-Fi decade of the 1950s. If anything, fly-fishing technology can be plotted in a kind of arc that tracks perfectly with the state of mankind's progress.

The Au Naturel Era of Angling with a Fly for Fyshhe (1700– 1930): Cane, feathers, fur, silk lines, horsehair leaders, canvas waders, hand-tied leaders, tweed.

The Industrial Revolution Era of Killing as Many Trout as You Possibly Can (1930–1970): Fiberglass, automatic reels, vulcanized rubber waders, tapered leaders, plastic lines.

The Space/Information/Digital/ Sensitive Male/Green Era (1970–present): Graphite rods, Microfibetts, poly dubbing, neoprene, GORE-TEX, fluorocarbon leaders, barbless hooks, catch and release.

The culmination of all the science in fly fishing seemed to reach a crescendo in the 1970s with two events: the publication of *Selective Trout,* by Doug Swisher and Carl Richards, and the creation of a line of fly-fishing equipment by 3M (Minnesota Mining and Manufacturing), a science-based company if there ever was one run by seriously Minnesotan engineers. This product line was named Scientific Anglers.

Scientific Anglers was and is a brand catering to those fly fishermen who were completely flummoxed by the whole flora- and fauna-centric nature of the sport. Gone was the guesswork and artistic flake component of fly fishing, and enter the Go to the Moon before This Decade Is Out ethos of the rational man. Want to catch a trout? Outwit something with a brain the size of a BB using the latest technology. Liberal-arts fly fishing is a stab in the dark, a one-way ticket to an empty creel. Scientific fly fishing is a mathematically demonstrable certitude, an IBM approach to a Baskin-Robbins problem.

My first exposure to this mind-set was when I was in junior high school in Minnesota and a kid who loved to fish (for anything). Trout on a fly became the Holy Grail; bass and panfish were for rubes and the cane pole, lawn chair, and bent-safety-pin set. The trouble was, catching trout was hard, way harder than throwing a chunk of dead meat on a gang hook into a lake and hoping some monster would happen by with its mouth open. I mean, you can catch trout that way. I've done it. But it's not that sporting, and it's certainly not scientific.

No, science is all, and my first exposure to scientific angling was through a kid named Lars.

Lars was into Scientific Anglers. It did not surprise me in the least when Lars grew up and became an MD. Lars' father was a PhD in some massively complicated scientific subject at the University of Minnesota. In my experience, the science gene usually skips a generation. Scientist fathers and mothers usually create children who are anything but scientists: Baroque flutists, performance artists, people who work in head shops, interpretive dancers, mimes, theater-lighting designers, bad novelists, and political cartoonists. But in Lars' case, the science gene not only went right to him, but with a twist: he would take his science gene and harness it to catch as many brown trout in the Kinnikinnick River as he could.

While I was stumbling through trout fishing using clumsily tied Gold Ribbed Hare's Ears, Lars was memorizing *Selective Trout,* learning how to tie physics-defying hackleless dry flies with the latest poly dubbing, and catching 23 fish for every accidental take I would get. He had the latest Scientific Anglers Weight Forward 6-Weight Silicone Lubricated line; the most sophisticated Scientific Anglers Specially Matched System reel, coordinated perfectly with his Specially Matched Graphite (what is that, like the stuff from a *pencil?*) rod; and a Scientific Anglers Specially Matched Perfectly Tapered leader and a Scientific Anglers spool of Perfectly Engineered tippet.

I almost felt like I was a country like, say, Belgium, deciding to jump into the race to the moon in late 1967. Some resources, some knowledge, but . . . uh . . . I wasn't a Scientific Angler. I was a Liberal Arts Angler, and I did not study very much. But not for long.

Liberal-arts angling was for losers, people who couldn't catch trout, people who simply were taken with the experience of fly fishing rather than the actual catching of trout. Suddenly, I wanted to be on the winning side, the victor and not the vanquished. I wanted to join the fly-fishing technocracy. I wanted to be an astronaut, not the poet laureate of the United States. I wanted to catch a lot of trout, fast.

I wanted to win.

So I learned science, or rather, was force-fed it. And so did all my liberal arts weenie fly-fishing buddies. Oh, sure, there were a few stragglers, the guys who would only fish with their grandpa's rod and didn't even care if they caught anything. But for the most part, people who could confidently recite Whitman, name the epic battles of the French and Indian Wars, do Latin conjugations, tell you the difference between *Henry VI* Part I *and* Part II, rattle off the names of the secretaries of state back to 1804, and otherwise *kill* you in Trivial Pursuit (minus the Science category) were now talking about loading properties and parabolas in rod design, the virtues and failings of titanium, the exact configuration of the proper diameters of tapered leaders, and, worst of all, entomology.

Entomology. Like, you know: insects. Or, as liberal arts people would call them . . .

Bugs.

We would talk about bugs, and, yes, I know that's a taxonomically incorrect term. Not literature. Not hermeneutics. Not deconstruction.

Bugs.

Trout, conversely, are not scientific in the least bit; they are intuitive, reactive, instinctive. Fishermen are, at best, analytical, persistent, rational, hopeful. They have dreams; trout have flashes of survival instinct.

Trout want to stay alive; that's their game. Fly fishermen stay alive in any event, unless they clock themselves on a slippery boulder and succumb to their own clumsiness. For a trout, the stakes are far different. They need to eat. Deception of an animal that has

no more higher brain power than a bowl of lime Jello is seeming child's play, and yet trout always have the upper hand. We devote hours and days and weeks and years to what? Getting a reaction from a barely evolved insect-eating machine? Some sort of excuse to be in the outdoors other than the mere appreciation of nature, a reason to stand in strong current flailing a wand while trout reject or accept our pathetic representation of their dinner menu?

Unscientific.

I have been trapped in more than enough quasi-scientific conversations about fly fishing that I have had no more business being in than a beagle would be discussing string theory. String theory, line theory, whatever. It all runs together. I make it up as I go along, and my liberal arts brethren nod knowingly, completely out of their depth, faking it all with panache. This is what men do: impart information that sounds really good, like a presidential candidate spewing policy cock and bull spoon-fed to him or her like a baby slurping Gerber's strained peas. Make it sound good, and the trout don't know the difference, right? Matching the hatch no longer must be a shot or a cast in the dark, a hope and a prayer on the end of a leader, an offering to the gods that we cannot see, hear, or perceive.

Matching the hatch is no longer a brown fly/gray fly question; it's an application of entomological game theory. Put out your theory, and it may prove to be true, like some economic posit made by some Ivy League charlatan armed only with a laptop and some cooked figures. The theory works when it works, and when it doesn't, well, it was only a theory. Next theory, please. Science is reliable, except when it isn't. Take a number. Place your bets, gentlemen. Black or red? Go on 17 or fold? The filly to place, the point spread is 9, the slugging average tells all, and all that. We can give 110 percent in fly fishing, and come back with .000.

That's science.

Can science explain to the nth degree of certitude why a Royal Wulff works and a Polywing Trico Spinner doesn't? Can science explain why your ear will be hooked by an errant cast? Can science explain why one day you'll limit out in a half hour in gale-force winds while on the next day, in the exact same spot with the exact fly and presentation, you'll actually *owe* the river trout?

Science cannot explain what faith and art can. A good friend once told me to use the fly you believe in. I did, and I caught a fish. That's not science, that's religion; it's either coincidence, blind luck, or karma. None of those are explained by science. Note that no one has started a fly-tackle company called Faith Anglers or Artistic Anglers. Who would buy their product in the Microsoft/Apple/Grumman/Boeing/Intel environment?

Me.

I am taking investors in Artistic Anglers right now.

Now hand me that bug.

FALLING IN

One of the great shocks of fly fishing is falling in; one of the greater shocks should be that you don't fall in all the time.

Think about it. You spend eight or ten hours in a river, ranging from strong current to 500-year-flood-level torrent, and most of the time, you don't fall in at all. You stay warm and dry, upright, and do not take the spectacular header that, based on the laws of physics, you should be doing about every 45 minutes or so. If you jumped into any given river, no waders, with no intention of going fly fishing, you would be taking a bath constantly, tumbling all over slimy boulders. But when you fly fish, this hardly ever happens.

People who usually fall in are what fly fishermen refer to as "aggressive waders." Aggressive waders are the guys who take the big wading chances, the Christopher Columbuses and Vasco da Gamas and James T. Kirks and Larry Craigs who explore and generally boldly go where no fly fishermen have gone before. I have heard more than one fellow angler described admiringly as an aggressive wader, like someone would describe an NBA point guard who specializes in technical fouls, or perhaps a really successful divorce lawyer.

"Well, you know, he's a trial lawyer—but he makes $7 mil per year. And he's gonna invite me over to his cabin on the Bighorn. And I won't be able to fall in, because he doesn't want the liability."

These aggressive waders tend to catch way more fish than the average angler. They take risks—they walk over tippy logs, they hopscotch through slippery round rocks, they walk a hundred yards out into very complicated currents that would challenge someone in a kayak, and more often than not will catch a significant percentage more trout than the guy taking it easy, who is sticking to the shallow gravel beds trying to make up for wimpy wading with long, insanely low-percentage casts over multiple rivulets of tricky back eddies and weird, convoluted chutes and pockets. In short, aggressive waders tend to win the day.

"How many did you get?"

"I got 23. I waded over to the far bank and swung like an orangutan on low branches."

"I got two. I worked the near bank."

Hmm.

However, aggressive waders will return from their little foray with, um, *evidence* that they had not, in fact, stayed dry. An unwritten rule is that falling in is a no-no, a sign that the fly fisherman is a clumsy spaz, and there is nothing other fly fishermen enjoy more than relentlessly questioning the coordination of a fellow angler. After all, fly fishing is a ballet sport, one where grace and fluidity and control are the hallmarks of the pursuit. When a fellow angler comes back with wet hair, a missing hat, and darker clothing than you remember that angler having worn when you last saw him (khaki is particularly telling), you know that the Ridicule Light has been turned on, and you may then proceed to mock your dripping colleague.

About 20 years ago, when I first moved to Oregon and started fly fishing, I went fishing in the North Fork of the Willamette near

Salem. My partner and I, the Immortal Phil Cogswell (we call him the Immortal Phil Cogswell to buck him up—because he doesn't like to acknowledge that he is, in fact, mortal—but hey, neither do I), were wading along, not really catching anything, when I slipped quite spectacularly—he on one side of the river, me on the other. I was in a fast current being carried toward a really deep hole that could probably hold a destroyer. The Immortal Phil Cogswell, a former Navy lieutenant (to tease him, we call him Ensign, which he immediately corrects) immediately fell back on his USN water-rescue lifesaving training and jumped out of the water, found what appeared to be a medium-size dead tree, and stuck it out to snag me as I was drifting toward The Abyss.

All I was thinking was, hold on to the brand new Sage rod. Wasn't thinking about drowning as my rubber chest waders filled up. I was thinking: this rod cost three bills. Obviously, as I am here to tell you about it, I grabbed the branch, was saved, and went on to win the Nobel Prize for Fly Fishing Humor in 1998.

That was my worst fall.

Another time I fell about 12 feet off of a huge log over on the North Fork of the Clearwater in Idaho. I wasn't aggressively wading, I was aggressively climbing, an entirely different level of trying to get to fish. It does, in fact, fall under the category of wading because I did cross the river. Falling into water is one thing, but falling into muck is another. I somehow lost my footing (again thinking, without much time to mull it all over as I was falling, *don't break the rod*), and landed on my shoulder in what was probably three feet of muck with the consistency of a milkshake. I looked like one of those chocolate-dipped Dairy Queen cones.

But I didn't break the rod.

Sometimes you deliberately fall in. Or, rather, I have made conscious decisions to get wet, in order to catch fish. Is this falling in? That would be a kind of ontological question that I am not academically trained to answer. I did this once, in the Deschutes, wearing a really nice new wool fishing sweater, and it was about 45 degrees outside. I saw a pod of working fish; they were out of range, and I thought—*I'll just fall in. Like this. Then I can get to them without admitting anything.*

Like it was kinda deliberate, kinda not. I needed to get over there, my friend Jim would have thought me insane to do this, and I needed to fall in as a cover story.

And, yeah, I caught one of the working fish. Don't ask about the new wool sweater.

Once you have fallen in, deliberately or not, the next set of questions that follow are:

1. Do I need to swim?
2. How do I get up/out?
3. Did anyone see me?
4. Can I cover it up?

When you fall in, one thing rushes through your mind (besides awareness of icy cold refreshing river water): Is anything ruined? We hang around the water all the time as fly fishermen, we use elaborate tools to get other objects into the water, and we are set up to be in and around water. However, we view it as a huge shock when we actually do physically immerse ourselves. We think, how could this happen? Why, God? Why did I get wet engaging in a watercentric sport. It's remarkable, once we do fall in, how many things we have that are completely ruined.

For example, flies.

I can't tell you how many times that I have fallen in the water with 1,239 flies in my boxes, forgotten to dry them out later, and then discovered expensive boxes filled with rust-covered chicken feathers and animal fur.

Why can't flies *stay* wet? It makes no real sense. They are, in fact, designed specifically to be in the water.

You are not.

Probably the worst thing about falling in is the fact that you have to then get up out of the water. After the shock of going from 78 degrees to 46 degrees in five-tenths of a second, you have to figure out whether you simply drift helplessly and hope to regain your footing a quarter mile downstream, or do you swim for it? You know you're not going to drown if you just elevate your legs and float on your back, but you have to have a get-out-of-the-water strategy if it's deep.

Falling in shallow water is almost worse because it just demonstrates that you've never done anything more athletic than throw a tennis ball to a dog. If you fall in deep water, you're a victim. If you fall in shallow water, you're a klutz. Falling in 18 inches of water among slimy boulders not only ruins your look, drenches your gear, and invites ridicule from your buddies, it hurts. You go down, there's the slightest resistance as you hit the water, a splash, and then WHAM—you slam your tailbone on some rock that perfectly inserts itself into your . . . you know. I once fell like that and couldn't sit right for six months. I went to the doctor and described my injury, and he just laughed.

"We can't do anything about a hairline coccyx fracture. Get a pillow for your office chair. And take a hot bath."

Weird.

It always comes back to getting back in the water.

FIFTY PLACES TO
DIE WHILE FLY FISHING

As we are all aware, those in the fly-fishing literary community anyway (that's you and a few other people—not me), this guy wrote this book called *Fifty Places to Fly Fish Before You Die*. I forget his name, but he has also put all out all these other books like *Fifty Places to Golf Before You Die*, *Fifty Places to Get Terribly Fat Before You Die*, *Fifty Places to Have Really Exciting Pedicures Before You Die*, and *Fifty Places to Go Die*. Oh, and 50 other titles like that. I would think he's made 50 million dollars, too. Not me. I wasn't that clever. I did have an idea called *Fifty Places to Go Buy a Book and Give Me Money*, but I can't get a publisher.

Aside from the mortal connotations of telling someone he has a finite amount of time to live, which I feel may scare off potential book buyers (I always tell my readers that they're going to live forever to bolster my own sales), I flipped through the book to see just where these places are. As far as I can recall, they were places like Montana and New Zealand and other places most of us can't afford to go to. I mean, God bless you if you actually go to those places, and I salute you, but I think most people just kind of dink around in their crummy little local stream and hope for the best. So I decided to compile my own list.

I think it would be far more realistic to compile a list of ways to die while fly fishing.

After all, most of the times I have kind of come close to dying, or at least really hurting myself, have been while fly fishing. That, and being in arguments with women.

1. Hook point in cranium.

2. Criticize fellow angler's gear; he throws it at you, hitting you in forehead.

3. Commit suicide when your box of 569 flies blows out of box in wind gust.

4. Suffocate in waders while it's 102 degrees.

5. Accidentally eat tasty-looking steelhead flies because you forgot CLIF Bar.

6. Bleed to death from brown trout tooth puncture wounds.

7. Cause massive drunken argument between friends over the merits of poly dubbing, which ends in gunplay.

8. Get lost on way to allegedly great spot, which is actually the La Brea Tar Pits; drive into tar.

9. Get hit in face with branch that broke off when you were pulling too hard.

10. Fall off log you were walking on, hit water, impale rod in your ear.

11. Die from boredom waiting for next hatch.

12. Trout wraps line around your leg, pulling you under.

13. Select size 24 midge, inhale.

14. Develop Chronic Repetitive Motion injury from casting, go into doctor's office, catch some crud from his garbage can.

15. Spot fish, make great cast, hook him on first try, die of heart attack from the shock of it all.

16. Decide to buy new rod and reel, see price, die.

17. See bait guys throw beer cans in river; walk over to them, give them a stern lecture about littering and recycling, and they put you in trunk.

18. Accept fishing invite from mob guy.

19. Wear bandanna and friends laugh, die of embarrassment.

20. Tie one too many flies, die from head cement jar fumes.

21. Walk into fly shop and ask where the poles are.

22. Tell your guide that he's doing it all wrong.

23. Give guide 5 percent tip.

24. Take float trip on River Styx (it sounded good initially).

25. Your wife gets VISA bill from fly shop run.

26. Tell your friends about the secret spot your trusted friend took you to; trusted friend finds out.

27. Small trout goes down your throat when you set the hook too hard.

28. Zinger comes back, 200 mph, at precisely the wrong angle.

29. Tell other fishing buddy about how bad his casting is.

30. Tell armed Fish and Game Warden that he has a funny name.

31. Make joke about how much buddy's SUV cost; he leaves you out in desert.

32. Book trip to New Zealand, land safely, take long car ride to river, safely; get attacked by rabid kiwis.

33. Fall in, inflatable vest goes off, knocks off your glasses; can't find car when you get back to shore, wander off into forest, walk blindly 34 miles; find town, find a diner, order the salad, contract salmonella.

34. Question the existence of God after a fishless day; lightning bolt comes down, hits you.

35. Jump into a hole while there's another guy in it, justifiable homicide.

36. Cast over another's guy line when he's reeling in, justifiable homicide.

37. Eat that nice trout from Three Mile Island.

38. Tease a guy at the hole about how his camouflaged truck with a lift kit looks.

39. A large caddis flies into your windpipe.

40. Tie up six dozen flies for a big trip and lose them, stroke out.

41. Decide it's a good idea to write a fly-fishing book, read reviews, stroke out.

42. A mountain lion in the vicinity smells you after you've been in the woods for five days and decides it's a tasty smell.

43. Go surf fishing for the first time and hook Portugese man o' war.

44. Drop your ninth new camera into the water, buy another one, decide to test it by accidentally taking a picture of someone in the Federal Witness Protection Program.

45. Make "just one more cast" with a graphite rod in a thunderstorm.

46. So thirsty, you decide to see what Gehrke's Gink tastes like.

47. Need polar bear hair for a pattern, fly to the Arctic Circle, find polar bear, and make the mistake of having lox for lunch immediately prior.

48. Go fishing with Dick Cheney on his ranch and he accidentally shoots you.

49. Kill someone after they say "tie flying," get executed.

50. Get a snag on the backcast, jerk back really hard, and drive the hook into a grizzly's nose.

SPARE THE ROD

Most of us own one of everything. House. Car. Lawn mower. Variable-speed cordless ⅜-inch drill. The fact is, most of us could get by with owning one fly rod, and that's how it starts. One martini. One potato chip. One fly rod.

Then we need more.

I discount all fly rods bought before an angler turns 25. Those simply don't count. Hardly anyone makes any real money before age 25, and then we're buying stupid stuff like food, clothing, shelter, transportation, insurance, and George Foreman grills. And, mostly, we can get by with owning one specific thing. Later in life, we wind up buying more than one of a certain thing, like hip replacements, but I can construct a really good argument that we generally can get by on owning only one of any given specific item.

Fly rods, of course, are different.

Fly rods are a necessity, right? Of course they are. One is, anyway.

The first real fly rod I bought was a Sage 690, and, in Oregon, I could certainly have gotten by using it virtually indefinitely for the vast majority of fly-fishing situations I would find myself in, such as not catching anything. Frankly, the only reason I even bought a Sage 690 was the insistent heckling of my newfound fly-fishing snot friends, who only fished with Orvis CFO IV reels and Sage rods. If you didn't have a Sage rod (as my main rod, I had a perfectly good Fenwick, which is probably now lost forever in my garage rod bucket), well, you were just not socially acceptable. It reminded me of that scene in *Crocodile Dundee* where he's getting mugged in New York, and this kid pulls a switchblade on him. Crocodile Dundee looks at the little knife, pulls out his machete, and says, "That's not a knife, mate. This is a knife."

I am not saying here that Sage rods are necessarily the be all and end all rods. They're not. But they are pretty nice. And, in 1984, all my fishing friends had them. I think it cost about $450, which was about three times more than the rod I had, which I considered to be astronomically expensive at the time. Little did I know that my future rod acquisitions would rival the GDP of China.

Having made the purchase of the Sage 690, which I really in good conscience could not tell my young new wife about—who was constantly nattering about things like new basinets (Oh! For bass? A net? Fine!) and baby food and crap like that—I then proceeded to use it. It worked perfectly fine, of course. I mean, I would haul the line in and out, it cast the prescribed distance, fish came in when they hit my fly, and it all worked according to plan. I had no real need for another rod.

Then I started noticing other people's fly rods. Some of the friends began talking about cane rods. Others said that their (insert prestige-rod manufacturer here) was really cool. It wasn't that my Sage 690 was bad—it wasn't—I just started developing, er . . . rod envy.

Get thee behind me, Freud.

The Sage 690, possessing what I would call a certain authority unnecessary for the disposition of 10-inch trout, became yesterday's

news, an autogyro, a stereopticon, black and white TV, last week's
People magazine. I determined that the best course of action would
be to get a lighter rod. Something really, really different.

A Sage 490.

Green. Whippy. Sassy. Impertinent.

And $500.

Once I had used the 490 for a few months (maybe it was days—
by this time, I had entered rod purchase delirium), I needed to move
on, again, and got an Orvis.

An Orvis 2-weight. Oh, but it was a *Western* 2-weight, because
I lived in the West. So I was able, yet again, to create a need. I tried
the 2-weight out a few times, but it seemed to be too . . . um . . .
what?

Old. That's the word.

Gee. Then I started reading about the Sage 596 (a 9½-foot for
a 5-weight). All my friends had moved on to the 596 by then, anyway, and I was beginning to fall seriously behind. How could I
possibly catch up?

By getting interested in cane rods.

Before eBay, one had to actually get catalogues, make phone
calls, scour ads in magazines, and receive mailing lists from sellers in
order to find a really nice vintage cane rod. After doing what seemed
to be enough research to actually write a college textbook about
cane rods, I settled on the Granger Victory, a massive relic from the
1930s that had the delicate touch of a 36-ounce Louisville Slugger,
was so slow that you could hear the *Jeopardy* theme music playing
while it loaded, and could work nicely as a telephone pole if you
could figure out a way to string wire from it. In short, it was useless.
My arm hurt after casting with it for more than six minutes.

I bought it anyway. Oh, and then I needed a lighter cane rod.
I managed to track down a Phillipson PowrPakt from the 1950s

(they said) that had two tips—one had a serious set (a bend in the bamboo) in it (remember sets? No, of course you don't . . . we have space-age materials now). It did have cool yellow wraps. I noticed that if I set the hook wrong, it was quite conceivable that I might have a handful of kindling where my cute little Phillipson used to be. I caught a 17-inch rainbow on it and promptly retired it. I was afraid that I would wind up with a nice cork rod handle with a 7-inch piece of cane sticking out of it.

Which created the need for . . . work with me, people.

Another rod.

By this time, I was dipping into the IRA, taking out huge home equity lines of credit, and borrowing against my life insurance to finance the Rod Acquisition Program, which was starting to have more cost overruns than the V-22 Osprey. One friend told me point blank that I had to buy a 10-foot for a 6-weight Scott in order to fish his property. I think that rod went for $600. Yes, I bought it. Of course I bought it. And I bought a Sage 3-weight.

I had to build that one.

Now, if you haven't built a fly rod, I can personally tell you in no uncertain terms that you have a better chance of building a working nuclear reactor out of LEGOS than you have of building a decent-looking fly rod. I mean, the line wraps alone made me insane for days, and getting the varnish on properly was the main problem. My rod, while it functioned perfectly (until I broke it— oops, no warranty—they always forget to tell you that part when you build your own rod), looked like it had been assembled by a drunken mole.

I took up backpacking in the mid-1990s, so of course I had to get an official Backpacking Rod. This was a four-piece, and I do not wish to reveal the name of the manufacturer for this reason: It sucks. The handle separates from the rod constantly. I have glued it about 60 times, and the last time I used it, I used this really cool new rod wrapping material I discovered called duct tape.

After several months of using all the previous rods I had purchased, I took note that the Fly-Rod-Making Industrial Complex had perfected the four-piece rod, which meant that I needed to upgrade what was now becoming a small fly-rod museum in my garage. I was amazed to learn that Sage and Winston had helpfully led the way with this new technology, which meant that I was morally obligated to purchase one from each company.

Now, let's recap and look at the numbers:

Sage rods: 690, 596, 396, 490 (two-piece)—and I inherited a Sage rod from my late friend, which I gave to my ex–brother in law. Oh, and the Sage four-piece.

Orvis: A 2-weight.

Granger: A 9-footer, cane.

Phillipson: A 7½-footer, cane.

Scott: A 10-foot for a 6-weight.

Winston: A 9-foot for a 5-weight.

Unnamed Lousy Rod Manufacturer X: a backpacking fly rod with duct tape.

Now, I have not even mentioned my other fly rods. My boyhood Phillipson 3M rod. A Fenwick. A cool old glass Shakespeare rod. I may have forgotten others. Oh, yeah. A rod I bought for my son which I think is a Scientific Anglers. There may be more. So let's add it all up:

That's 16 rods.

That I can remember.

There could be more. I need to check.

Yesterday, I went to the fly shop by my house. It's Kaufmann Streamborn, which is a major mail order outfit as well. They had the full complement of the usual suspect sizes and brands . . . and

Spey rods (I don't have one of those—yet). I even picked a few of them up and shook them a little bit, just to see if they had that ineffable something that says "Put me on your credit card." Picking up a rod and shaking it a little bit is kind of the fly-rod equivalent of kicking the tires on a new car—something to do that tells you nothing, really. Who has actually bought a car after kicking the tires? It's so 1920s. The weird thing was that I told the salesman I was going to a certain lake to try out the bass fishing there, and the salesman informed me with authority that I should probably get an 8-weight. Huh. Maybe I could just duct tape my 6-weight to my 2-weight and call it an 8.

I have landed 12-pound rainbows on my Scott 6-weight, so I was a little skeptical. I told him so. He looked at me sadly the way salesmen do when you have made a sensible decision not to get what they want you to buy. In fact, I didn't even pick up an 8-weight and shake it a little bit, just to see if it, you know, felt *plausible*. Because if I got an 8-weight, I would then feel compelled to get a new reel to go with it, and don't even get me started on new reels. Or line. I did look at the new reels. Some meth heads had stolen all my CFO IVs out of my truck—I think they nailed me for about two grand worth of reels alone, and I, for some sick reason, have been getting by perfectly fine for the past three years on the three replacement reels I got (one was a Bauer—nice, looked like a Nikon). The glass case was filled with fabulous Bauers, Sages, and Rosses. I just couldn't pull the trigger.

So I didn't get a new 8-weight.

That would have been excessive.

IT

B lanked.
You caught nothing.

No takes, no rises, no fish, no nothing. How do you go on?

You can tell that it's gonna happen. You've been fishing all morning and you haven't seen a thing. You have changed flies 27 times, you have switched from dry flies to nymphs to Woolly Buggers, and you are now seriously considering lifting up a log or boulder in search of a couple of night crawlers or maybe even a grub. You have gone from 5X to 6X to 7X. You have tried dead drifts, roll casts, weighted flies, twitching, stripping, dancing, prancing, praying, dredging, screaming, yelling, swearing, weeping, and lying.

Nothing.

It's a bad feeling that comes over you like some depressive cloud, a growing awareness that you have no home equity, China now makes everything crappier and exports it to the United States and charges twice as much for half the merchandise, the Democrats and Republicans not only lie to you, but act like they think you think you have no idea what the inning and the score is, and you are never, ever gonna get your garage in any kind of order. You are not going to catch anything. Anything. At all.

Ever.

At least on this trip. And if you are just 30 miles from your house on some local dribble, just messing around, hoping that some trout is going to yawn and suck down your Olive Whatever, you think: well, it's important that I'm just out here in God's Creation and fishing. I don't care if I do catch anything. Once you start thinking that it's important that you don't catch anything, well, by God, you're not going to catch anything. It's like a doctor telling some poor patient that he has Advanced Trichonometriosis of the Pancreatic Duct or something that sounds like that, and there's nothing anyone can do about it, and the five-year survival is Zero Point Zero, and you better call your lawyer, your financial guy, and then a courtesy call to your minister. But if that same doctor says, hey, you've got this weird-ass disease, but I was just flipping through the *Journal of the American Association of Pancreatic Duct Therapists* and saw something that may work, what the hell, and we're gonna just give it the old college try, you might make it to collect Social Security. Same deal with fishing. It's all attitude.

One of my best fishing buddies calls it Using the Fly You Believe In—a theory of religion and fly fishing that actually seems to work sometimes. I have two flies I believe in: a black Woolly Bugger with Flashabou and a little contraption called a Deer Hair Spider Emerger, which is a kind of all-deer-hair Humpy with a black thread body and a grizzly parachute. Try tying some up sometime in 16 and 18—nobody sells them. You will see the light, fast. This thing works all the time when nothing's going down, you can't buy a strike, the hatch is not being matched, and you just go with the fly that has worked before, and bang—fish on. Attitude.

When you first start fly fishing, whether it was in 1959 or last year, you have so many early experiences that end up as not only goose eggs, but as actual humiliations, that you probably have way more skunked days than you have lots of fish days. The thing is, at least with me, if I even catch one fish, or even get one take, I can walk away and say, well, I turned one. If I catch a few, I can walk away with my head up. I worked the situation, figured something out, caught a few, and the day is saved.

I recall one trip where I had driven four hours in a driving rainstorm in Oregon—we have those—got to the river at a primo time of the year, with plenty of time for the hatch to come off, and I turned the water into a meringue. I mean, I whipped the river until it had a head of foam, tried every fly in the box, and saw NO rises, got NO takes, caught NO fish. I still remember it, ten years later. The thing is, now, I almost always catch at least one. I work all day, put it in the right places the right way, and I will almost always catch something, even if by accident. That wasn't always the case.

In a way, it's amazing that I didn't just quit fly fishing by my mid-20s. I distinctly remember having the feeling that I was going to shift my tender mercies and attention to what I called non-outcome-based recreation. Skiing was what I decided on. My default mode sporting outdoor activity now is hiking and bike riding. You can't screw up a hike, except when you make a wrong turn or turn an ankle. Skiing you can screw up, like if it's too cold, you leave the ground momentarily and land on your rear, or find that your outfit is the wrong color that year. Bike riding, same deal: get on the bike, roll. Usually no screwups unless you fall off, which almost never happens anymore—except for the time my front wheel came off at ten miles an hour downhill in 1988. But there are so many things that can go wrong when you're fly fishing that it defies categorization. Virtually everything can go wrong when you're fly fishing, which, in turn causes you not to catch trout.

The top things that can go wrong: wrong fly pattern, wrong tippet, wrong presentation, wrong cast, wrong positioning, wrong river, wrong state, wrong state of mind. Wrong, wrong, wrong. It's like the space program. There are so many things that can go terribly wrong with so many microscopically small systems, it's amazing that we can even figure out how to get the astronauts to the launch pad in a minivan, let alone get them up boldly where no man has gone before. Fly fishing is a series of systems that can fail at any time, any place, anywhere, and you feel like you have no control at all. And when it all seems to work, and trout are being caught hand over fist, you get to congratulate yourself on your brilliant analytical skills. And when they aren't being caught, you can sit back and blame them.

"The little swine. They're just being temperamental. I have done everything correctly." The fact is, pal, that if you had done everything correctly, you wouldn't be having that little exculpatory conversation with yourself.

It's hard to keep your game face when you begin to have that gnawing feeling that you're going to have a bad day. The realization starts creeping in about lunchtime. You're sitting on a rock with your friend, and you say, "What do you think?" And he says, "Geez, I don't know, man—we've used the right fly with the right tippet and the right presentation and between us we've got 68 years of combined fishing experience, and it ain't happening."

And you don't have to say what "it" is.

"It" is whether you're catching fish, or not. During a *Hexagenia* hatch on a lake, I once said to my eldest son, who has next to no interest in fly fishing (I have tried to teach him, tried and tried and tried, and he just isn't interested), "It's happening." He must have been nine or so, and he knew exactly what I was talking about when I said the word "it."

David Letterman has this routine that I love called "Is It Anything?" He and Paul will watch some hapless amateur hour performer come out and juggle Chihuahuas or play "Misty" on a chain saw, and Dave asks Paul, "Paul, is it anything?" Paul usually responds, "No, Dave, it's not anything." Then Dave says, "I agree—it's nothing."

They might as well be fly fishermen.

When it ain't happening, what can you do?

Well, there are the standard responses, and if you are any fisherman at all, you know what they are and what the odds are that it's going to work. There is the declining order of effectiveness, and everybody knows what you try when nothing's happening.

1. Change flies.

2. Change to a smaller tippet material.

3. Go wet.

4. Throw an open can of Spam into the upper part of the pool.

If none of those work, say by four o'clock, I usually declare some sort of defeat, pull off the waders, unstring the rod, and move. Moving is critical. If you just stand in the same spot for six hours and throw everything in your vest at the trout, then you just know that it is simply not going to go anywhere. After almost 30 years, I can still recall this great vignette in Tom Wolfe's book *The Right Stuff*. A test pilot is declaring an emergency. He screams into his microphone: "I've tried A, I've tried B, I've tried C, now what?" The ground controller says something like, "Shut up and die like an aviator." There are moments when you just have to shut up and die like a fly fisherman.

Sometimes you just have to assume the position when you can't catch anything. It's difficult, of course, and no one likes to quit, particularly fishermen. It is particularly difficult to quit not when you are fishing that stream 30 miles from home, but when you have driven 14 hours (one way), stayed overnight in Walla Walla in the same room with your friend who snores, spent $220 on gas, bought the recommended flies, and maybe you even got a special new rod just to fish that specific stretch of water, and it's in some Reliable Nationally Recognized Great Fly-Fishing State like Idaho, Montana, Colorado, or Wyoming, and you still come up empty-handed.

That hurts. No, more than that.

It happens.

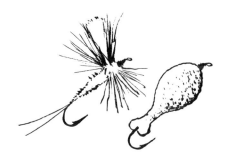

ONE MAN'S MEAT

In 1984, Dick Thomas, aka "The Geezer," and I went fishing in Oregon's Fall River. Dick, a former managing editor of the *Rocky Mountain News* and assistant managing editor of *The Oregonian,* among other things, was called The Geezer because one day, when he was steelheading, a mutual friend of ours ran into a kid coming out of a trail down to the Sandy River. He asked the kid if there was a man fishing down below, and the kid says, yeah, there's some old geezer in there. At the time, Dick was about 47 years old.

That would make me a geezer, too, at this writing. More than a geezer.

Anyway, The Geezer and I headed down to the Falls Hole. I am not going to tell you where it is—some things have to remain sacred—but suffice it to say we were armed. Heavily. We were packing the George Bodmer Nymph.

The George Bodmer Nymph is a pretty obscure fly. Dick picked up the pattern from a guy in Colorado, I guess, and it looked suspiciously like a Gold Ribbed Hare's Ear, but with some red in it . . . I think on the head. We positioned ourselves right below the falls, threw in between the two major flumes where there was a little slack water, and Dick used this finger over finger, excruciatingly slow retrieve. It took about five minutes to get the fly back, but this specific retrieve resulted in the most unbelievable day of brown trout fishing I have ever experienced. Even The Geezer agreed it was a banner moment in the history of American angling, and he had fished Colorado in the '50s and '60s. So the George Bodmer Nymph would land in the prescribed slack water, thrown in precisely where it needed to be, and we would take turns stripping it in, and WHAM. Brown on.

We must have hooked or caught 40 browns between 12 and 17 inches. All day. Arms tired, wrists throbbing, fingers raw, the slow strip and the Bodmer produced one nice fish or at, minimum, a take on every other cast. There must have been hundreds of browns stacked up like planes over O'Hare in a thunderstorm. We could not miss. We took the biggest browns and threw them on a stringer. By the end of the day, we had limited out in a way that was reminiscent of those 1930s sepia-toned photographs of men standing next to 389 trout in ascending order of size. We looked like the guy on the old Wright and McGill hook packages. We threw them in the cooler and drove back to the Fabulous Oasis Motel, featuring green carpet on the walls. I suppose it was to keep the noise level down when the local Bend gentry were having midday assignations.

As we emptied out the cooler onto my driveway in Beaverton, I looked at our catch, frozen on the asphalt. I felt a pang of regret. Prior to this fish slaughter, I had reveled in a big stringer of dead fish. It was physical evidence that I had Killed Them, Wiped Them Out, Knocked Them Dead. As I surveyed the damage, I decided that I would not kill any more trout if I could avoid it.

Now, I am not saying I haven't killed a fish since then. In mountain lakes that freeze over, brook trout are dropped from airplanes or helicopters specifically for fishermen to catch and eat. They ain't gonna make it through the winter, anyway, so have at it. I have caught and eaten many helicopter-delivered brook trout. I have also killed a 16-inch brown that was bleeding profusely from the gills—that was in 1991, and I took it home and ate it immediately, with some fried potatoes.

It really didn't taste very good, but I figured it was part of the deal: you kill, you eat. You do not cryogenically preserve them in the freezer like Ted Williams' head for future generations to deal with. As a teenager, I kept a bass I had caught in 1972 in the freezer for about four years. I would routinely show him off to neighbor kids and admire him myself sometimes when I was feeling low. Eating that brown trout I caught meant that I was going to be at the top of that food chain, since I still have opposable thumbs, even if they feel sore a lot of the time. I still have the head of a four-pound bass I caught in 1974 in my garage.

Yes, it's gross.

But I think that foul-hooked brown was the last fish I killed.

After I had purchased the obligatory CATCH AND RELEASE WILD TROUT license plate frame, I was ready to test out my new regimen of not keeping any trout. The first time I went out, I didn't catch anything, thus relieving any need to indulge in catch-and-release self-congratulation. But as I moved forward, I went barbless, stringer-less, creel-less, and net-less.

I kind of missed not carrying a net for a long time. Fishing and nets are primal; they are inextricably, historically attached, and I found myself reaching for a net that wasn't there many times, like a missing limb. Once in awhile, when I have to declare a big fish emergency, I will find myself putting my hand behind my back to grab the net that isn't there. Then I remember that I actually don't need to net or beach the fish, except if there's a camera around.

I find myself photographing fewer and fewer fish, because I can remember them, anyway.

It is hard to return a trout to the water and not be awestruck by its beauty; you are gaping at the red spots on the brown, or the little blue speckles on the brookie, or the iridescent stripe on the rainbow, and you just want to hold it forever, like a diamond or a Rolex, and just marvel at it. Even as I would kill trout 25 years ago, I would never think: gee, I want to eat that. I want to frame it. My first impulse now is to get it off as fast as I can. That isn't through instinct, it's through rote training and negative reinforcement.

A good friend of mine once told me that he kills a fish once in awhile to remind himself that it's not a game. He possesses a more finely honed killer instinct than I do; he's a stockbroker and a golfer and they are more that way, anyway. But I get what he's saying.

People for the Ethical Treatment of Animals has turned its attentions to fishing. Assuming that all the members of PETA do not eat meat, any animal-based food of any kind, wear leather, or otherwise indulge in anything resembling animal hypocrisy, I still assert my own right to sit at the top of the food chain, and I want to preserve the resource not only for myself, but for others, too. So I catch and release. Does a fish feel pain? I don't know. Maybe. Does a mayfly feel pain when the trout eats it? Do I or should I care? There is a lot of injustice in the animal kingdom. The big things eat the little things. I try not to worry about that sort of thing, because I figure it's out of my hands. We fish to indulge in a primal urge that we don't really understand in our Drive Thru/Fast Food/Supermarket paradigm, and, at least in fly fishing, we can throw them back to live another day. There is no catch-and-release duck hunting.

But it would be cool to try it.

MARQUETTE

In 1962, when I was about two, my family moved to Marquette, Michigan, in the Upper Peninsula. If you have never been to Marquette, well, it's very near Ishpeming (the next town over on U.S. 41), which is the home of Robert Traver, who was one of the great 20th century fly-fishing writers (*Trout Madness,* among others). Robert Traver's real name was John D. Voelker—he was a Marquette County prosecutor and a former justice on the Michigan Supreme Court. Of course he was a fly fisherman . . . he was a lawyer. He also wrote the book *Anatomy of a Murder,* based on a case he prosecuted and won (his guy got off on an insanity plea), and which was later made into a movie starring James Stewart and Lee Remick.

One of my enduring regrets in life was not executing my plan to attempt to fish with John D. Voelker. He died in 1991. I still own the Marquette telephone book with his name and phone number in it. Up there, in the 1960s, we all still had five-digit phone numbers, and there his is, on page 34 of the Ishpeming section:

"Voelker John D Deer Lk Rd, Ishpeming, HU 6 6934."

If you had a Marquette, Michigan, phone book from January 1968, there it would be, I swear.

After all, I was a Published Fly Fishing Writer/Humorist/Cartoonist, and I arrogantly assumed he would welcome my attentions with open arms. I actually read a piece that was written right before Voelker died by a writer who wanted to do that very same thing, and did. It was an interesting piece; turns out that "Robert Traver" was pretty eccentric, smoked a very stinky cigar the whole time the writer was around him, and took him out on his private pond to fish for brook trout—I think between them that they caught only one brookie on the order of eight inches. It reminded me of this other book this guy wrote a few years ago, where the writer fished the *entire length*—like, 100 miles or something—of a river in the Upper Peninsula—and caught one small brook trout. I guess it was a journey of midlife discovery, although, in retrospect, I think the author would have preferred a few more fish and a little less personal midlife discovery.

At least he got a book out of it. And, no, I didn't have the guts to call John D. Voelker, either—and then he died. I saw that his house in Ishpeming was for sale a few years ago, and they wanted some pittance for it, like $65,000. Not to say that it crossed my mind to buy it—I am the kind of person who would do something like that, but after a quick check of my savings account, factoring in the airfare (Portland to Chicago to Detroit, puddle jumper to Marquette), I came to my senses quickly. I hope whoever bought it knew what it meant to own Robert Traver's/John D. Voelker's house.

Marquette was, at the time, a Valhalla of fly fishing; I haven't been there since 1972, so I can't speak to how it is now, but I suspect it's still pretty good fishing up there. It was settled by the usual complement of hard-working Norskies, Swedes, Germans, and Finns (the largest minority group) who were brought in to work the iron-ore mines (the longest-running Finnish language television program is still broadcast on WLUC-TV, hosted by the same guy

I saw growing up there in 1965, and I am pushing 50 years old). My dad grew up around there in the 1940s, and so he knew his way around the birch woods and streams when we moved back there. My earliest fishing memory was of being taken up to a series of ponds called "Three Lakes," which ran right next to a railroad trestle. I caught many sunnies, and once, on a tiny Zebco, I hooked a bass that must have been close to two pounds—a massive fish for a five-year-old armed only with a three-dollar rod.

When you're a child, the microscopic awareness of the world you have is gradually expanded by the environment in which you're raised, and I was raised in a fishing house. I began to hear the names of the rivers around Marquette, and they are still evocative to me to this day: the Carp (which ran about a mile or less from my house), the Dead (finally, a river with a built-in excuse for lousy fishing), the Chocolay, and the Laughing Whitefish. These were all places that my dad would discuss in what I am sure were extremely tedious conversations to my mother, who was not an outdoors person, unless you count sitting around on the back patio smoking cigarettes with Rosemary Arnold outdoor living.

My dad would bring home trout from these rivers, or perhaps from trolling the mouths of the rivers in a 12-foot boat in Lake Superior. Fishing remains perhaps one of the few reliable common languages I still share with my dad, other than his oft-expressed frustration/glee about my inability to use hand tools to any useful effect.

"Put some soap on that screw . . . THEN drive it in. No, no. Your other left." And so on.

Yeah, okay. I try.

As fathers of that generation often did, they were probably most accomplished at pointing out how you were messing up, since they had come back from serving in World War Two and Korea and were busy building the booming postwar economy. You, on the other hand, were a lazy baby boomer who couldn't put soap on a screw properly.

I did, however, learn how to fish from dad, and we did do that quite a bit. In so doing, we managed to talk way more than we would have had we not shared fishing as a common interest. I wouldn't say my dad was laconic, but he was of Norwegian and Swedish second generation parents (his father, Elmer, would ask his wife, Mabel, a question in Swedish, and she would answer in Norwegian), and these are the kind of people who do not convey any more information in a sentence than is absolutely necessary. I mean, they don't ask you *how you are* and *how you're feeling*. They convey hard data. I suspect that I had more in-depth conversations with my dad about fishing plugs and flies than I did anything else.

Dad never really picked up the fly-fishing bug like I did, and it is rather astounding because there is very little to do in Marquette, Michigan, except fly fish. Wait, there's deer hunting. And, man, did he deer hunt. Some of my most horrifying childhood memories were of dead deer hanging up in our basement, and it was like living in a deer morgue. Oh, he made a passing run at fly fishing, but mostly he stuck to the tried and true Midwest fishing orthodoxy of Ford Fenders, Rapalas, Bass-Orenos, Jitterbugs, Hula Poppers, Creek Chubs, mother of pearl spoons, Daredevils, Mepps spinners, bobbers, night crawlers, minnows, and Helin's Flatfish. In a way, I miss that kind of fishing because there's always a little action on the end, particularly when you're a kid.

"Dad, I think I got something."

"No, it's just the way it's supposed to move."

"No, it's wiggling. I think I got a fish."

As in space, when no one can hear you scream, in fly fishing, no one can really be sure if you have a bite or not, particularly if you're nymphing. As a little boy, there was absolutely no question whatsoever that you had hooked a sunnie or a bass. Bobber down, fish on—pretty self-explanatory. A small trout is an almost electric sensation in your hand, like a joy buzzer. I suspect with my dad, a fish was a fish. There was no hierarchy, no morally superior tactic, no better species (excepting suckers and carp): just get it hooked and get it in.

Fly fishing is all about hierarchy. A rainbow is better than a brown, a brown is better than a brookie. A bass is debatably not necessarily better than a walleye or a northern. Each has its charms, but no walleye fisherman sniffs at a bass fisherman the way a dry-fly angler snorts derisively at a nymph fisherman.

Marquette is surrounded by beautiful small streams, with sandy bottoms and deep cutbanks, or, at least, that is my childhood recollection. A simple handline worked quite well in many situations. Not having fished the UP extensively, and knowing full well there are famous, world-class rivers that I have never fished, this is not meant as a full discussion of the joys of Michigan fly fishing the way serious anglers approach it. I'm just saying there was a trout stream within walking distance of my house, and it had all three species in it. I still recall catching 4- or 5-inch trout, bringing them back to my mother, and her saying, "You kept that?" Hey, it's a trout. I'm a child. Of course I kept it.

My dad's forays into fly fishing were tentative feints; he had a Shakespeare rod and a Pflueger Medalist reel, nothing fancy. He tried fly tying, and he ordered all his material from Herter's, a now-defunct mail-order joint that was one of the definitive outdoor establishments of the postwar era. I remember the dubbing wax and the big needle he used, the vise, some feathers and hooks in a wax bag, which were safely stashed in his desk drawer. Again, a low-level commitment.

Someone he worked with, a man named Rod Jacobs, had made a major commitment, indeed, a lifestyle choice. Rod Jacobs was single, lived out in a cabin, had a few Labrador retrievers, and was, in my dad's eyes, The Luckiest Man on the Face of the Earth because he could hunt and fish at will. My dad was too busy doing too well at his job running a lab for the United States Forest Service in Marquette, and when you do well at something in the government, the first thing the government does is make you stop doing that, move you to Washington, DC, and turn you into a bureaucrat. Which they did. And he was a damned good bureaucrat. But he never did any more scientific research, which was tragic—in his day, he actually discovered quite a number of fungi of the northern hardwoods, and he loved being in the lab. I do not recall that he even touched a petri dish while in DC, but he did testify before Congress pretty often, which is a different kind of petri dish that I think he enjoyed much less.

But in Marquette, Rod Jacobs loomed large in my conversations with my dad.

"Rod caught a 6-pound brown the other night at two in the morning." This is what dad thought he should be doing: stalking brunos at 2 AM instead of being a research scientist, but, instead, Rod was doing it. I am pretty sure Rod wasn't real high in the USFS food chain, but he was an expert fly tier. And, for some strange reason, Rod quit fly tying and gave me all of his fly-tying stuff in the early '70s. Well, this was like hitting the lottery to me, and I wound up with tons of rooster feathers, Herter's hooks (they suck), dubbing material, congealed wax, and all manner of stinking, rotting fly-tying stuff that any sane aspiring fly fisherman would want. I still think of this as the best windfall I have personally ever scored in my entire life, and, to this day, my favorite smell is not apple pie out of the oven, a baseball diamond, barbecue, or roses: it is fly-tying materials.

Rod must have gotten a girlfriend if he didn't have time to tie flies. I still tie flies from Rod's stuff, and every time I tie I think about him, even as I only knew him in passing.

My dad's fly-tying efforts were pretty rudimentary: some Woolly Worms, olive, and that's about it. We may even have some around somewhere. In examining these flies as a teen, I could tell that he clipped the hackle. A no-no.

I am quite certain that my dad would say, if awakened at three in the morning, that the critical mistake of his adult life was leaving Marquette, and that he should have become a plant pathology professor at Northern Michigan University. How could I disagree?

One day, dad came home and told us that we were moving to Washington, DC. My mother was ecstatic—the shopping in Marquette consisted of a mail order Sears store, a five and dime called Jupiter, a department store that I cannot recall the name of, and a downtown main drag that ran about six blocks.

So, in March 1968, Dad loaded us up in the Chevy Impala wagon, and I bade good-bye to the Carp, and the Dead, and the Chocolay, and the Laughing Whitefish, and fly fishing. It was not exactly the best time to move to Washington, DC. After Martin Luther King was assassinated, I stood on the hill in Roslyn at my dad's office building and watched the most important city in the world *burn*, and then Sen. Robert F. Kennedy was killed weeks later. I went to his burial at Arlington Cemetery.

This was not what they had taught us would happen in Mrs. Goodney's class at Fisher Elementary School. The system was all supposed to be as straight as an avenue laid out by Pierre L'Enfant, solid as marble, as linear and inspiring as Federal-style architecture, and Congress making wise and just laws in concert with a steady and statesmanlike president with white hair. The 1960s really hadn't gotten rolling yet in Marquette. I think we were enjoying late 1949.

I then spent the next 20 years trying to get back to a place where I could reliably fly fish again.

You can't go home again. No doubt. But you can move to Oregon, and that was even better.

To this day, I dream about Marquette, Michigan. I can see the buttercups and the bluebells, the birch trees and the massive snowdrifts, the ice floes on Lake Superior, and I can still hear the foghorns from Presque Isle pier as the massive iron-ore ships dock. I still can see, in my mind's eye, the little brookies swimming on the bottom of the sandy streams, and I wander, looking for a good place to drop a line in the Carp River.

Someday, when I am old, I will go back. I think I can even find the trail upriver by the power station. It's right by the Tiroler Hof Motor Hotel on U.S. 41. I can remember sitting by our black-and-white Zenith television set, 40-foot-high ice floes on the shore of Lake Superior, children with long-forgotten last names, blueberries, my neighbor's Edsel, a drive-in called Hamburger Heaven, neighborhood dogs, foghorns, and icicles the size of King Arthur's sword. Mostly, though, when I think of Marquette, I think about trout.

I miss it. But mostly, I miss the fact that I didn't really get to really learn to fish Michigan well. Someday, I will walk up that trail by the Carp and try to catch the two big browns my dad nailed on a grasshopper in 1964.

But I will use flies.

WEATHER OR NOT

I have spent a lot of time having weather discussions. I grew up in Minnesota, where the weather can, in fact, kill you. I mean, Minnesota has Death from Above tornadoes, blizzards that get a running head start over the Great Lakes or the Canadian prairie and bury your house in a glacier in 24 hours, and, last but not least, petrifying cold that can turn your house into the back of a Good Humor truck in minutes if your furnace craps out. We had an AM radio station in the Twin Cities, WCCO, which, during tornado season, seemed to be strictly devoted to telling people to go to the southeast corner of their basement with their own personal body bag. Sometimes, for fun, I will listen to WCCO online, and they'll do the temperatures every hour: "It's 2 above in St. Cloud. Faribault reports 6 below. All molecular motion has ceased in International Falls." This is in July.

In Minnesota, the weather has an absolute way of telling you that it's that time of year to stop fly fishing. Once the snow starts flying, God is telling you to get out the ice fishing shack, watch the Vikings, and kill deer with a rifle. We don't talk about the weather in Minnesota, we issue alerts to each other.

So I have become practiced in the fine art of weather chat. In Oregon, the weather is comparatively quiet. I once knew a woman who was a television meteorologist, and she and her husband, also a television meteorologist, moved to the more dramatically stormy Dayton, Ohio, because they thought the weather in Oregon was boring. Now, I can tell you no one voluntarily leaves Portland for Dayton, unless they have an excellent reason for doing so, like having committed some sort of felony. I know for a fact that they didn't commit any crimes against humanity (aside from working in local television news), but I do think they also left because our Portland ABC affiliate began running a feature called "Bob the Weather Cat."

Oregon weather is predictable. You may have heard that it rains here, and if it's not doing that, it's showering. Sometimes it drizzles. A nice day would be a slight mist. So the weather conversation runs along the lines of, "Hey, do you think it'll rain for a 17th consecutive week, or should we quickly evolve into a water-breathing animal?"

In fly fishing, weather is a ubiquitous topic, and sometimes about as compelling as cocktail party conversation about scuds. Believe me, I have been to some cocktail parties where scuds would be a welcome conversational gambit. Still, it needs to be discussed, and every fly fisherman has his own personal completely unscientific theories about the effect of weather on the fishing. Being someone who is not a trained meteorologist (I consult Bob the Weather Cat instead), my mind starts converting into tapioca pudding when I hear the word "isobar." So I don't know anything about this other than how I think weather affects fishing. Here is my take:

Sunny weather. I have caught fish under these conditions.
Cloudy weather. I have caught fish when it's cloudy.
Rainy weather. I have caught fish when it's raining, absolutely.

Snowy weather. I have caught fish when it was snowing, too.

Tornadoes, hurricanes, typhoons. I have not caught fish under these conditions.

So, I guess what I'm saying is this: you tell me. You tell me how it all works. Because I have no idea what the real practical relationship between weather and fly fishing is, except for:

Windy weather. Not only do I hate windy weather, I can reliably say without a doubt that windy weather is a huge pain in the ass if you fly fish. Everything gets more . . . everything. Knots start, flies hit you on the back of the head, nostrils get torn, lines get tangled, leaders snarl, and small regional wars start in far-off nations. You can't make anything resembling a decent cast, and if you do, by accident, the trout are not only not feeding, they're vacationing in the south of France.

Unless, of course, it's just a little windy. Then the caddis blow off the bushes into the river, and the trout key on them, and you have the right size and color caddis, and then you nail them. Unless you don't.

Define a little windy. Well, as you can see from this isobar, if a wind is gusting lightly from 3.3 to 5.6 mph, and if that wind is generally variable (plus or minus 4 percent), and there are the right number of isobars, then you are in meteorological business, my friend. Fish will be caught. Unless it's blowing in the wrong direction.

What about barometric pressure? What about it? People insist this has a causal relationship to fishing, but, frankly, I am not convinced. I am not convinced because I have been skunked under all possible conditions. Plus, this is a math thing. No one can really explain barometric pressure. Anyone who has a barometer is completely baffled by it.

Flat light? See, I am a big fan of flat light. If I could pick one weather condition, it would be flat light. Is flat light a weather condition? I don't care. But I do like flat light. Flat light seems to encourage mayfly and caddis activity. I like just enough illumination to see what I am doing, but not enough illumination to highlight my flaws, like a fluorescent light in the bathroom.

Just what is an isobar? I don't know. Stop asking about isobars.

Okay, what about fishing in tornadoes, hurricanes, and typhoons? Hey, have at it. I could envision circumstances under which each of these particular weather conditions would work to your advantage in fly fishing. For example, a good Category Three hurricane could very well assist you in your cast, assuming that it was at your back. Tornadoes could cause tangles in your leader. Typhoons are counterclockwise hurricanes, and might be useful in putting a little extra action on your wet fly, should you want to do that, counterclockwise.

Anyway, the weather.

The weather also dictates what you wear when you go fly fishing. Before 1980, when they had only three clothing materials: wool, cotton, and Daczylon (I made that last one up), there wasn't really much of a discussion about what to wear when you went fishing. Fly fishermen wore red plaid wool shirts and funny hats—maybe jeans and a T-shirt. But there wasn't any of this so-called technical fiber around, even for people who were launched into space. When Al Gore invented GORE-TEX, there was a major breakthrough upon which all Americans could agree, but what this did was cause the price of fly-fishing weatherproof clothing to skyrocket. Not only that, it caused many fly fishermen to consider the concept of color coordination.

If the weather was lousy, you put on an incredibly uncomfort-able rubber jacket, or, if you were rich, you got a Barbour jacket, which is covered in . . . um . . . wax, I guess. This made you look like a real live Atlantic salmon fisherman, of which there are about 13 in the entire world. I got one; I felt like I was trying to look like Prince Charles—not my favorite look, plus my ears don't go with the jacket at all. I suppose His Highness's ears could be used as an emergency weather shelter in a pinch, if he and I were out Atlantic salmon fishing, which I only do a few times a week.

I also have depended on the use of a poncho, which makes you feel like Mama Cass Elliot trying to execute a roll cast in a bath-room stall.

Now, of course, things are different. There are fly-fishing shirts that aren't red plaid, have little military epaulets that make you feel like you're in some kind of trout-based paramilitary unit, and come in any variety of light pastel colors that simply have to go with that darling little bandana you now have to wear when you're photo-graphed. They make short jackets so that the bottom part doesn't get wet, hats that protect you from the skin cancer generating unit in the sky we revolve around, and special wicking underwear to help out when you've lost control after you lose the Big One.

Is the fishing best right before a thunderstorm? Yes. The fishing can be excellent right before a thunderstorm. Then you get struck by lightning because you are whipping a graphite lightning rod around. This can be bad. For example, getting struck by lightning can really mess up your backcast. Fused leader material, there is the smell of burning deer hair, your fly vest has been rendered into a plastic ball, and your cute little bandana has been seriously singed.

What about fly fishing in the snow? Well, first off, if you are in a heavy snowstorm, you can pretty much forget being able to differentiate the snowflakes from a really heavy PMD hatch. A photographer friend of mine once took a shot of me fishing in a snow flurry 25 years ago on the Deschutes, and sold it to a magazine as a Yellow Sally hatch. Guess the photo editor must have had a cracked loupe, or perhaps was simply on deadline. Snow angling is difficult; ice in the guides is a major problem, and your line winds up looking like a candle in about 15 minutes. Some of the largest fish I have ever caught have been in snowstorms, which only slightly mitigated the fact that I was wackier than a bag of hammers for even attempting such a feat. If you get caught in a snowstorm while you're fishing, fine, but deliberately going out and fly fishing in a snowstorm is a sign of a real problem.

Return to the subject of sunny weather. Okay, sunny weather can either be good or bad, depending. Sunny weather can warm up the water, but, then again, you don't want it to warm up too much. Sunny conditions are also very pleasant to fish in, but I wouldn't know about that, living in Oregon. They can also rapidly turn your youthful skin into looking like the back of a grizzly cape.

And if you start seeing isobars in the sky, that's a real bad sign. It could mean that you're hallucinating. Or worse.

It could mean you're from Minnesota.

FLYING BLIND

One of the most perplexing things about fly fishing is actually having to make a call about what kind of fly to use. For many of us, matching the hatch looks like the way to go, and a quick survey of what's happening on the surface followed by a dumpster dive into our fly box is sufficient. But many times, the old rules of match the hatch do not apply. Any serious fly fisherman carries several hundred to several thousand flies. I think I am usually carrying about five fly boxes. I have never counted, but my guess is that I have about a thousand flies ready to use on my person, with another thousand or so sitting in the truck, conveniently not located anywhere near me in critical situations, such as when I need them.

My backup fly boxes have all sorts of bizarre patterns that I invariably don't use. They're an archaeological dig of dragonfly nymphs, Chernobyl Ants, bass poppers, Bitch Creek nymphs, and a host of other flies the guy at the fly shop SWORE would work. My experience has been that, usually, the recommended fly at the fly shop kinda works, sometimes, but you can wing it and do just as well half the time. All of these sit in silos in my truck and fly bag, waiting to launch on warning, and yet I almost never get around to using them. They sit in a small traveling fly museum, and I am the curator.

Some anglers belong to the light fly/dark fly Presentation School, on the theory that it's all about where you put the fly and how you put it there. Listen: I have been there and done that, too. I have watched trout rise all around my *perfectly* presented fly, cast in the *exact* spot in the feeding lane, and I have *direct* physical evidence that the fish are looking upward, and . . . tada! . . . nothing. Present This. Then I finally figure out what the masking hatch is, or that they're actually feeding on some size 24 midge, make the change, and I will then get a take. I'm not saying presentation isn't, say, 40 percent of the game, because it is, but I would feel safer with the right pattern and a bum cast than with the wrong pattern and a great cast. I would describe the sensation I have when using the wrong fly as exactly the same feeling I have when my tie doesn't go with my suit quite right. The tie is great, the suit is great, the knot is great, and it's . . . wrong. I know, lose the suit and tie.

There are still a lot of rivers in the United States where it doesn't really matter precisely what fly you use. A Large Famous Western River I fish all the time is a good case in point. The fishing is crazy, particularly in the fall. Which one? It's one of the rivers on the left side of the Continental Divide. For some reason, it is perfectly okay—in fact, preferred—that you use a Renegade.

A Renegade.

That's right. I wrote R-E-N-E-G-A-D-E; the dumbest pattern there is. It imitates nothing. It's not cool to look at. It can be tied in two minutes and ten seconds. And on this river, a Renegade is the fly of choice, which is akin to going into the bar at the Waldorf Astoria and ordering Pabst Blue Ribbon in a can. It just feels so wrong, so Paris-Hilton-in-Vegas-watching-an-Elvis-impersonator trashy, and yet the Renegade is the go-to fly. I feel actual profound . . . what? . . . shame. Shame. I feel shame in using the Renegade. But there it is.

Other flies should evoke similar shameful feelings, but they don't. For example, I unabashedly advocate the Royal Wulff, the Woolly Bugger, and the Yellow Humpy, all incredibly gaudy and silly flies, and I feel absolutely no guilt in so doing. The Royal Wulff is what it is: an attractor pattern. You put on a Royal Wulff, and you know exactly where you're at: desperation . . . the drunken slob at the bar trying to get a date at closing time. And it works. It works all the time. The Woolly Bugger is lethal, and it looks like it would be, but I get more flared nostrils and dismissive snorts when I profess my deep and abiding love for and use of the Woolly. The Woolly is a hand grenade: them or us, the fullback at the two-yard line with three seconds on the clock. It works, too. Brilliantly. The Yellow Humpy is also an asinine Christmas tree ornament that can make it all happen when nothing else seems to. You might as well tell fellow fly fishermen that you keep a few Mepps spinners and a jar of PowerBait in your vest.

No, I don't, to answer your question.

Now, conversely, matching the hatch is a mug's game, which is one of my friend David Reinhard's favorite phrases, and he employs it all the time when we're fishing. "Don't cast there—it's a mug's game." I usually respond, "Yeah, it's a death trap, it's a suicide rap, we gotta get out while we're young." Then I go ahead and do whatever it is he says not to do. I like to match the hatch when I can, and I usually carry enough flies to get within field goal range of matching the hatch, but I am nowhere near some anglers' precision skills. Mostly, I can come up with a cream-colored fly around the same size if I need to, but I am always forgetting to load up at the fly shop on those; I'm usually too busy getting more Royal Wulffs, Woolly Buggers, and Yellow Humpies.

I have never advertised myself as a great fly fisherman, or an expert. A-Plus-Level fly fishermen always have 10 to the 6th power flies that exactly correspond to their indigenous waters, plus every single river within a 2,000-mile radius of their house. In contrast, I may have the right fly, but it could very well be rusty because I forgot to dry off the box the last time I dropped it in the water. Furthermore, I am woefully undereducated when it comes to entomology; I know something about it, but . . . look . . . I have a degree in U.S. History, which means I could probably Google what James Madison's favorite flies were, but that's about it. Otherwise, I am not exactly the first guy you should call up to find out what *Ephemerellas* are coming off. However, I do know how to identify quite a number of reliable fly patterns.

All I know is this: I like flies with deer hair.

Yep. It's that simple.

Deer hair is your friend. It floats, it's natural, and the color is right a lot of the time. If I were limited to one material, it would be deer hair. Sorry, deer. Many of you will have to go hairless for my preference, but to me, deer hair is the new black. Or maybe it's the new elk hair. My favorite fly is composed almost entirely of deer hair. Grizzly hackle is my second favorite material. Grizzly looks like deer hair. Of course, I would choose the most expensive hackle material there is, but it goes so well with deer hair, and it makes any fly look like a natural, even if you have a chenille optic body with rubber legs, the grizzly can give it just enough natural oomph to make it work. My third favorite material for a fly is Golden Retriever tail fuzz, but it's a way distant third.

When you're actually confronted with going into a situation in which you have no idea what you're doing, like a marriage, you have to adapt quickly to the rapidly changing environment. Fly fishermen call this prospecting. How do you prospect? How do you just pull a fly out of the hat if you don't really know what's going on? Well, I usually just go over to the bank, sit down on a rock, and quietly weep. Then I get up, go into my fly box, and make an educated guess about what kind of pattern could actually work. I look at my pocket hatch guide, I get out my little net to pick up what's floating downstream, I take the water temperature, I consult the *Farmer's Almanac* for the solunar tables, and then, and only then, do I start drinking.

Once I have selected that special fly that I know will work, I then carefully present it in all the right places based on my extensive experience and knowledge of other rivers I have fished before. After I have put the fly in all the usual suspect places, covered every single foot of water perfectly within 60 feet, it is at that moment that I will get a strike as I am accidentally dragging the fly on the swing. "The swing" is a technical term fly anglers use to obscure the fact that they caught a trout entirely by accident.

I know, this is a weird conversation that only fly fishermen can have. We are actually discussing animal hair and chicken feathers, and it's a serious conversation. Please don't bring this up at the water cooler, unless you want a nice padded cell with the man who thinks he's Franklin Delano Roosevelt, and the other guy who swears—*swears*—he can get the exact frequency of Area 51 in his fillings, and/or call in an alien mother ship with a duck call.

I've seen him do it. It's pretty cool.

And when he puts deer hair and grizzly hackle on his duck call, watch out.

MAYBE I'M ALL WET

One of the things I find fascinating about fly fishing is the notion of moral superiority.

Over a fly.

Not to get all metaphysical or anything, but what is a fly, anyway? For the sake of discussion, let's break a fly down into its constituent parts:

1. A short piece of bent wire, with a sharp point on one end and a little loop on the other.

2. Some fuzz.

3. Some feathers.

4. Sometimes, other stuff.

Now, having stated the obvious, let's break it into two categories: dry flies and wet flies. Dry flies consist of all of the above materials. Wet flies also consist of all of the above materials.

And yet, almost without debate, dry flies are considered to be morally superior to wet flies. Period. I have actually had to referee fights between grown adult men over the question of whether a dry fly is better than a wet fly. To me, it's a matter of preference, obviously, and the purpose of fly fishing is to catch trout.

Isn't it?

I know, I know, it's more than that. To some, fly fishing is all about the experience, the outdoors, the ambience. In a lot of ways, trying to define what fly fishing is all about is kind of like trying to determine the existence of God. If you get an answer, beautiful, but it's more about the journey, anyway. I interviewed John Gierach in 2008, and he pretty much said to me that fly fishing was about being in pretty places. Really, that's about the size of it.

And yet, the debate remains.

I have averted eye contact with people when I have mentioned that I was using a dropper. My fellow anglers have made all sorts of remarks in the tone usually reserved by U.S. attorneys having a little chat with Mafia wiseguys. Sometimes, if I tell them I was using a Woolly Bugger, I feel like I've just bought myself a one-way ticket to a bulletproof-glass witness booth at the World Court at The Hague.

INTERNATIONAL PROSECUTOR: Your honor, may it please the court that the prosecution has entered into evidence a size 6 black Woolly Bugger, and that DNA evidence has conclusively tied this fly to the defendant.

ME: I can explain! There wasn't any hatch, I was just prospecting, I hadn't gotten a strike in seven hours, it was 47 degrees, and I swear I won't do it again.

INTERNATIONAL PROSECUTOR: The court will note that the defendant has offered no defense whatsoever.

Look. I know that dry-fly fishing is fun. It's cool to see a trout take a fly on the surface. It's dramatic. But I just feel like using a

wet fly shouldn't be a cause for me feeling like I need to go into exile. For example, a few years ago while fishing in the (DELETED FOR NATIONAL SECURITY REASONS) River in (WESTERN STATE), I was offered a challenge: catch a trout in front of the group I was camping with. I had five minutes. Five. Now. If I won, I got five dollars. Who would walk away from that, particularly if a person had a beer and a quarter at lunch?

So I tied on a black Bugger, knowing that this was almost like cheating, like using a night crawler at a hatchery or throwing a stick of dynamite in a farm pond. Maybe not that bad, but still, you know the feeling, because the Fly Fishing Social Arbiters had long ago decided that my method was really so comically déclassé, so gauche, so tawdry, that I might as well have said, "Hey, look at this Rapala with a pork rind I tied on." The thing is, I wanted to win the five bucks, there was an audience, and, well, I knew the Bugger would probably work. I was also pretty sure that if I went with a nice little dry fly that I probably wasn't gonna win the bet. Just a hunch.

So I threw the Bugger out into the current, worked it hard all over the drift, and I was watching my watch. Two minutes, three, four . . . no strike. Stripping wildly, putting all sorts of action on it, and kind of wishing that, in retrospect, I had tried a dry, since the wet fly wasn't really doing anyth . . .

BOOM!

Fish on.

The wet fly works, again. Oh, yeah, and give me the five bucks.

When I brought the fish in, I am pretty sure my audience didn't see that I was using a Woolly Bugger, and when I held it up, well, let's just say that points were taken off because I was using a wet fly. This kind of bothered me, because the terms weren't exactly clearly stipulated. But, in a way, the terms are always stipulated: *A dry fly is morally superior to a wet fly.*

And I knew it.

But why? Why? Why did I let myself fall into this stupid paradigm? I could blame the Big Liberal Fly-Fishing Media Conspiracy, but that would be too easy. I let myself fall into it because operant conditioning is highly effective.

On the other side of the fishing aisle are our brethren, the Lure and Bait Guys. The LBGs never trouble themselves with the Yale Debating Society Niceties about one method of catching a fish being better than the next:

ME: What did you catch him on?

LBG: A sucker minnow harness. And then I clubbed him over the head with a 36-ounce baseball bat.

ME: Oh. Wow, he sure is bleeding (wiping spatters off your pastel Patagonia bonefishing shirt) a lot.

LBG: Yeah, need to put him on the stringer (while simultaneously gutting him with a Rapala fillet knife that could take off your fingers without any hesitation at all).

I know, I know. Fly fishing is more about the art rather than the catching, and it is truly amazing to see a really nice dry fly take. There's a saying that goes like this: "If you give a man a fish, you feed him for a day. If you teach a man to fish, he'll eat for life. If you teach a man to dry fly fish, he will go completely insane and then starve to death."

The debate always seems to be between dry flies and wets, but you never hear any fly fishermen having a really animated argument about the moral superiority of a Clouser Minnow versus a

Mickey Finn. I have never heard an argument about the relative merits of a Pheasant Tail Nymph versus a Scud. In Oregon, there is a river where the olive scud is the Fly of Choice, and if you tell a dry-fly angler that you are using an olive scud, it's like you told them that you live in the backseat of a 1979 Chrysler K car. I agree that it's a lousy car, but if the fly was tied on a fly vise, presented on a 5X tippet, then it's not like you were using Vienna Sausages.

Those might work. Or you could probably tie them up in deer hair.

Moral high ground is slippery. If you want to fish dry, more power to you. I prefer it, being an official fly-fishing author and all, and therefore have a certain reputation to protect. But I hate the feeling of being in the United Nations General Assembly screaming about the morality of a piece of wire and fur.

I have often wondered what the debate is like over in Bass Nation. Is there a school of thought that plastic worms are tackier than a beautifully hand-painted plug? Is a Mister Twister ethically better than a Rapala? Do fistfights break out over the use of worm inflators versus worms that are allowed to float naturally? What about bass boats versus rowboats? Mealworms versus crickets? Minnows versus leeches?

I can make the call on minnows versus leeches. Minnows. Easy. No call at all. Leeches are disgusting.

My guess is that they don't have those types of arguments.

Fly fishing is incredibly nuanced, and it is practiced by a lot of anglers who are nuanced people. Nuanced people like to have big arguments about small things. Henry Kissinger once said that faculty senate meetings were so heated because the stakes were so low. It's about the only thing I have ever agreed with Henry Kissinger about.

I wonder if Henry Kissinger is a fly fisherman?

IS FLY FISHING ELITIST? A QUIZ

One of the more troubling aspects of fly fishing, to me, is the perception that it's elitist. Elitist is kind of a relative term, and there are a lot of fly fishermen who also enjoy spin fishing just as much. For the record, I grew up in Minnesota, where a politician who wasn't photographed holding up a gleaming walleye or northern pike wound up with 36 percent of the vote, and man, he better have caught it on a big minnow, leech, night crawler, or a treble-hooked lure the size of a pipe wrench. In fact, when I was 13, *TIME* once ran a cover of Minnesota governor Wendell Anderson lifting what I felt was a rather anemic northern on a stringer. God knows if he actually caught it. Wendy Anderson was also a hockey player, so he pretty much cornered the remaining Minnesota demographic between his photo with a northern and his ability to shoot a piece of rubber into a net. There are worse qualifications for being governor of Minnesota. Pro wrestling comes immediately to mind.

Growing up, I didn't think of fly fishing as elitist at all; it was kind of like the story of white kids and African-American kids growing up next to each other in the segregated South, playing together happily, and then being informed that they had to hate each other as adults. So I bore no class warfare baggage in my pursuit of fly fishing at all; in fact, when I grew up, the first thing I did when I made any money at all was to buy the most tricked-out fishing boat I could afford.

Now, I love boats as much as anyone, and yet, as any boat owner (or former boat owner) knows, they can be an expensive cash suck and a massive headache. I owned several boats, and one was quite impressive: a 17-foot Smoker Craft with all the doodads: two livewells, pedestal seats, a flasher *and* what was then a sophisticated graphing depth finder, and three engines (a 50 hp Evinrude, a 5 hp Evinrude, and a foot-control electric trolling motor).

I used the big boat for awhile, then I noticed that I was mostly storing my rapidly accumulating fly gear in it. A sign. I sometimes miss having a real boat, but I just prefer the relative simplicity of fly fishing. I still do have a small PennYan rowboat, but I do not use it that much; it's probably 60 years old, and sounds very creaky and fragile. It was the first boat I was ever in, and my dad restored it. I have fly fished in it, but mostly it hangs in my garage, waiting to be taken out.

Now, boat ownership may or not be elitist. Do you own a 55-foot sailboat, or a 17-foot Smoker Craft? Fly fishing *can* be elitist. The question is, is all of fly fishing elitist? Are all fly fishermen elitist? Here's a quick fly-fishing elitism quiz:

Q: When I go fly fishing, my preferred location is:

A. The stream that runs by my house.

B. The stream that runs by my Swiss bank.

Q: **When fly fishing, I enjoy the company of my good friend:**

A. Who works as a Chevy truck mechanic.

B. Warren Buffett.

Q: **If I'm not catching anything, I will:**

A. Change to a smaller fly and a lighter tippet material.

B. Have the responsible parties blackballed from my club.

Q: **I vote for candidates who support:**

A. Clean water initiatives.

B. Clean water initiatives that don't interfere with the toxic waste I dump from my factory.

Q: **If I am having issues with my casting techniques, I often rely on instruction from:**

A. My other buddies on the trip.

B. Lefty Kreh whom I have flown in on a C-130 I control as part of my leasing agreement with the Central Intelligence Agency.

Q: **If I break my rod, I simply:**

A. Go into convulsions, swear, and have to divert money from checking for five months to buy a new one.

B. Cash in one of the gold ingots I have lying around on the floor of my beach house in Majorca.

Q: One of my favorite people with whom I discuss fly-fishing experiences is:

A. Some guy I know named Larry.

B. My old contracts professor when I went to Harvard Law.

Q: When I fly fish, I sometimes daydream about:

A. How much I really want to get a 3,000-watt Honda generator.

B. My favorite Pinot Gris.

Q: When I break off a really big trout, I will sometimes exclaim:

A. "Shit!"

B. "This is a piscatorial defeat of the first magnitude."

Q: When I go fly fishing, I get in the driver's seat of my:

A. 1998 Tahoe with 103,456 miles on it.

B. Gulfstream G5.

Q: If I make a bad cast in front of my friends, they will:

A. Throw a beer can at me.

B. Move to have me expelled from the New York Athletic Club.

Q: I have fished with guides and enjoy:

A. Learning all their tactics and techniques, hearing their jokes, and watching masters at work.

B. Treating them like indentured servants.

Q: My dad used to take me fishing all the time in:

A. Minnesota.

B. Tweed.

Q: Sometimes, when I am alone, I feel envious of anglers who have:

A. A new bottle of fly floatant.

B. A new bottle of Glenfiddich.

Q: Catch and release is for people who:

A. Aren't hungry.

B. Have disposable incomes above $400,000 pretax.

Q: When I fill up the gas tank on my Suburban, I feel:

A. Crushing chest pain.

B. Around in my pocket for my black American Express Card.

Q: Typically, when I go to the fly shop, if I see something I like, I will:

A. Carefully check my budget, ask myself if I REALLY need it, and then, having made a considered judgment, will pass because I have kids in college.

B. Get the rights to the patent, and then set up a production facility to manufacture it.

Q: If I get a snag up in the brush, I will:

A. Carefully walk back to where the fly is hung up, drop the branch down, and slowly backing the barb out of the wood, remove the fly.

B. Have my people handle it.

Q: I got interested in fly fishing in college, when I was hanging out with the guys at:

A. A frat house at Boise State.

B. Skull and Bones.

Q: When I need to pick up some flies, I generally run over to:

A. The fly shop by my house.

B. Orvis headquarters in Manchester, Vermont, which I just bought in a hostile takeover.

Q: When I see someone fishing in my spot, I deal with that by:

A. Walking downstream a little bit and finding a new hole.

B. Buying up all the riparian rights along the entire length of the river, filing a restraining order in U.S. District Court, and having the angler arrested by U.S. Marshals; having him audited by my friend in the IRS and exposing his personal life by leaking photos of him and his love child to the *National Enquirer.*

Q: To me, an ideal lunch while fly fishing would be:

A. A knockwurst sandwich, a bag of Cheetos, and a Dr Pepper.

B. Catered.

GETTING YOUR KID TO FISH WITH YOU

I have three children, ages 21, 18, and 15. They do a lot of different things in life and have many different skills. For example, my oldest son, Eric, has a photographic memory, an ability to master any video game extant, writes beautifully (he got one wrong on the verbal portion of the SAT and is still puzzling over what it is that he missed), plays bass guitar (he has three of them), and is pretty deadly at Ping Pong. My daughter, Julia, is an international model (she has been to Singapore and New York City a few times already), is a varsity lacrosse goalie, writes and draws very well, and has a knack for picking up musical instruments and figuring them out. My youngest son, Bobby, is an accomplished drummer; plays the guitar well; is a fine basketball player; loves other sports like golf, lacrosse, baseball, and football; has the dry delivery of a stand-up comedian (as do they all, actually); also excels at the aforementioned video games; is a fairly diligent student; and is, well, cool. Like, really cool—unlike me at 15. Now, of course, at 48, I am so cool and the future's so bright, I have to take LIPITOR.

But not one of my kids fly fishes with me.

Eric was, of course, the first one to get the full immersion program. I knew I was in trouble when I handed him a Sage rod at age three, and he jammed it into the gravel, breaking it off at the handle. You should see what he did to the model railroad set I built for him when he was five—let's say that Mr. Expensive Choo Choo got jammed into the fake lake with the real sand, and that was the end of the electric train era. He punctured some waders the second they were taken out of the box, and generally has no knack for or interest in fly fishing at all. He can't tie knots, doesn't like standing still, and generally is temperamentally and physically completely unsuited to be a fly angler. Oh, sure, he has caught a few fish in the way that kids do. I have taken him to a really productive private lake, where he somehow managed to catch the largest fish on the trip (kids do this constantly, to let you know it's not rocket science), when he wasn't constantly having me untangle his leader, tie on his fly, and generally acting like he wasn't into it in the slightest bit. That isn't his fault; I have no more interest in playing *Grand Theft Auto IV* than I do in learning how to use a whip finisher. It's just the way he's wired.

The thing is, however, that I would really like to have a kid fish with me now, as I approach, you know, death.

I took my youngest son, Bobby, fishing earlier this year, and he seemed to enjoy himself, but I wouldn't say that he's been exactly begging me to go since. In a world where there are so many other visual and sensory stimulations for a teenager, fly fishing seems 1890s quaint in comparison. I felt like I was handing him a View-Master instead of a cable TV remote.

"Uh, Dad? What's this?"

"It's a View-Master, son. You put the cardboard circle with the slides in it, move the handle up and down, and pretty pictures of Yellowstone or funny Disney characters show up in the eyepiece."

"Oh."

I loved View-Masters.

Anyway, contrast this with my efforts to expose Bobby to golf, a sport in which I am laughably incompetent, and Bobby has become a poster boy for the nascent golfer. He wants to go every weekend, wants a new driver, complains bitterly over his score, watches all the tournaments, and generally exhibits all the telltale signs of a future golfer, like obsession and a strong desire to make $1.2 million a year in stock options. No plaid, yet.

As for my oldest son, he rightly observes that fly fishing is not his bag—too much small motor control and silence. He does, however, like to sit with me while I fly fish, and will read a book and pleasantly exclaim when I catch something. That's something. I enjoy his company, regardless. And I am glad he's reading books, a low-tech hobby in which I have decided to make the big bucks. Ahem.

I held out some early hope for Julia and fly fishing, but she has only gone a few times, and the fishing has been—as it is usually when I try to teach someone to fish—"off." I took her down to this little dribble of a tributary, thinking she would connect in some pocketwater. I mean, you don't even have to cast, just hop around on rocks and dap the fly over the holes. Nothing. If I went on any given day other than one on which I needed to catch something, I would probably catch eight or ten small rainbows, but the day I want to teach my daughter, well, there was nothing happening. I am not even sure we were fishing in water at that point. It was a clear liquid of some kind—kerosene, gin, Sprite, I don't know really what it was—but it wasn't holding any more trout than your bathtub with the faucet running.

Fly fishermen, to a certain extent, are born, not made. Take the bathtub. When I was a kid, my mother bought me a little plastic fishing pole with plastic fish, and I would put them in the down-stairs washtub or the bathtub and try to snag them. Sure, I was raised in a fishing environment, there was a fly rod in the house, trout were caught, but the fundamental fact is that I was compelled to even try to catch plastic fish. That's nature. When my dad took me fishing at age five, I was into it, big time.

Now, don't ask my dad about trying to make me into a hunter.

Okay, you asked.

My dad tried to make me into a hunter (and a research scientist, but that's a different book). We lived in Michigan and Minnesota, and seeing dead deer tied to the roof of our car and the cars of others was a common sight. So, in 1975, when I was old enough to take the Minnesota Gun Safety Course, I took the Minnesota Gun Safety Course, as did virtually all of my friends. I passed without serious injury to myself or others. My dad handed me a rifle (a Ruger .44, I guess it was—we were in heavy brush, no scope) and drove me up to Koochiching County, Minnesota, where we then sat for the next four days in below-freezing temperatures, waiting quietly for a deer with suicidal ideation to happen by. None did. Dad used to get one every year in Michigan, and he got a few in Minnesota without me, but I never saw a doe, buck, fawn, or anything else on four legs except a squirrel on the three or so deer-hunting trips I've been on. And I know it bugged my dad—a lot—that I never took to it. Nor did I take to duck hunting, or grouse hunting, all of which I have done.

Not my bag. But if you want to do it, I am not some urban, whining limousine-liberal-PETA Goody Two shoes. If the resource is managed properly, state game laws are observed, you're wearing orange, and don't fire your rifle at my house or car or me while I'm hiking, then lock and load. When I was 16, my dad and I got into a dramatic argument about deer hunting. I observed, correctly, that bowhunting seemed more of a challenge (I didn't say more sporting, I said more of a challenge—to me, bowhunting is the hunting equivalent of fly fishing), and he observed that I didn't display the requisite blood lust necessary to properly enjoy the sport. I agreed, sarcastically, and, well, let's just say we didn't talk to each other for three days after. I think he was more hurt by my lack of interest in deer hunting than he was about my juvenile observations. We haven't hunted since.

Later, we did go skeet shooting together, which I did enjoy and did many times in the 1990s, and now my son Eric does that. I loaned him my dad's Charles Daly over and under, gave him some shells and clays, and said, in a sage voice, "Have fun. Don't aim at your foot, internal organ, or anyone else's foot or internal organ."

My kids, conversely, have tried on numerous occasions to interest me in video games. Had video games existed in 1973 (I remember getting *Pong,* which is now probably going on eBay for $3,000), I am sure I would have been right there, staring at the screen and trying to sneak up on James Bond or an F-18 or a street thug, and losing my virtual life in 30 seconds. Some of the video games I do enjoy, like *Jeopardy,* but that doesn't really count. I find myself watching *NBA Live 2008* and *Madden* like they were real games, except the games go by without beer commercials, which is highly disorienting.

A few years ago, a company came out with a fly-fishing computer game, which I did try a few times. I was even able to fish a virtual Deschutes, which was filled with large virtual trout and where I was able to make a great number of virtual inaccurate and incompetent casts with virtual wrong-pattern, too-large, wrong-color flies on virtual too-fat tippet material, whereupon I would get virtually skunked, just like on the real Deschutes.

Eric picked up on it immediately, for some reason. He would catch three-pound trout, make seemingly improbable upstream-round-the-bushes-sidearm-slingshot roll casts, get drag-free drifts for 50 feet, get three fish chasing one fly, and generally make me feel like I was sitting on a folding lawn chair with a cooler and cane pole with a bell on the end.

I gotta get a different controller.

So, I assume that someday, one of my kids will come up to me, maybe when I'm 60 or something, and say, Gee, Dad, the guys at work are going on a fly-fishing trip, and maybe you could lend me some gear. You know, give me some pointers. You used to fly fish. You wrote those books.

By that point, I will have given up on fly fishing and be happily immersed in racking up points on *Grand Theft Auto XLIV*.

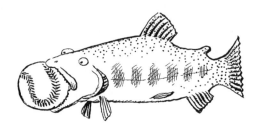

THE AMAZING SIMILARITIES
BETWEEN BASEBALL AND FLY FISHING

While Americans think that baseball is the national pas-time, fly anglers would disagree. In fact, the Committee to Replace Baseball as Our National Pastime with Fly Fishing has issued a report saying that baseball and fly fishing could actually merge, if all the lawyers can work out a final agreement. Following are the results of that study, which was commissioned by Baseball Commissioner Bud Selig and Fly-Fishing Commissioner Jack Ohman (I just appointed myself to that, because it sounds cool and way better sounding than a political cartoonist). Baseball and fly fishing have remarkable parallels, and a draft report of our study is available online at www.baseballandflyfishing/merger.org.

BASEBALL	FLY FISHING
A.Rod	A rod.
Water cooler	Cool water
Pop flies	Popped tippets
Funny caps	Funny caps
Dropped flies	Dropped flies
Nothing happens most of the time	Nothing happens most of the time
Blind umpires	Blind casting
Cut off man	Cut off hackle
Successful about .250 of the time	Successful about .250 of the time
Shortstop	Short strike
Game of inches	Game measured in inches
Catch-and-release ball	Catch-and-release brown
Colorado Rockies	Colorado Rockies
Adopted by East Coast intellectual types and overanalyzed by academics	Adopted by East Coast intellectual types and overanalyzed by academics
Field of Dreams	*Field and Stream*
Turgid books by amateurs microscopically parsing the ephemeral	Turgid books by amateur entomologists microscopically parsing the *Ephemerella*
All tied up in the ninth	All tied up for the ninth time on log
Hits, errors	Hits, errors
Rain delays	Rain delays

BASEBALL	FLY FISHING
Sacrifice	Sacrifice checking account
National and American Leagues	Izaak Walton League
Seventh-inning stretch after about two hours	Seventh lost fish after about two hours
I don't care if I ever go back	I don't care if I ever go back
Switch hitter	Switch flies
Screaming crowds on Opening Day	Screaming crowds on Opening Day
Fifty percent of the game is half-mental	Fifty percent of the guides are half-mental
One, two, three strikes you're out	One, two, three strikes you're out of the one fly that works
Was really great until 1965	Was really great until 1965
Say it ain't so, Joe	Say it ain't slow, Joe
Bench filled with losers	Fly-tying bench filled with losers

INTEL

There is this program in the Pentagon called Total Information Awareness. It's part of the intelligence community creepshow that threatens to turn this country into a national security totalitarian throw-the-Bill-of-Rights-into-the-garbage-disposal dictatorship, but I digress. TIA has this bizarre logo with God's Eye staring out of a pyramid, like the dollar bill, except the eye is now a $2 billion satellite instead of God's. Anyway, if you guys are listening or watching, well, remember this is just a humor book about fishing, for God's sake. I'm joking. Please, I am joking. You know, like when I say I caught 22 fish and I really only caught 19. I must have lost count. Anyway, fly fishermen have the same kind of Total Information Awareness arrangement, if a bit more subtle and lower-tech.

We call it intel.

Intel is critical to any successful fishing trip, and if the intel is gleaned in low voices in darkened rooms with the shades drawn and loud classical music blaring to drown out potential eavesdroppers, that makes it even more fun.

Intel is roughly divided into three categories: truth, rumor, and absolute horseshit.

Let's start with truth and the standard to which that truth is vetted. Truth would be something like, "My brother-in-law owns 135 acres in Idaho. It's a private river, and he catches 19 inchers in there on badly tied Royal Wulffs all the time. In fact, over Labor Day Weekend, he caught 13 fish in an hour. It's a lead-pipe cinch." What this stuff has to do with lead pipe is still a mystery to me, but you know the Truth is out there when someone uses that phrase. The truth of all this can be determined with certain code words and phrases, such as "my brother-in-law." A brother-in-law is very unlikely to lie, unless he wants his portion of the garlic mashed potatoes completely eliminated at Easter, and that goes double for the deviled eggs.

If he's lying, then there will be serious, immutable consequences, like beating him at gin rummy or making sure that his wife knows that he spends an inordinate amount of time at a place known simply as "Jiggles" off Route 34. I am not suggesting that one reveal this sort of information, it's just useful to have it on ready reserve—just in case verification is needed. Yes, this kind of thing is illegal, but this is fly-fishing information we're talking about here. Blackmail isn't blackmail until it's actually used. Before that, it's like kicking up the national security threat to Orange . . . it could happen, but if we are vigilant, it won't. God forbid.

Truth also sounds plausible. What is plausible versus implausible? Plausible is a 30-fish day and a couple of 17-inchers. I mean, that does, in fact, happen. Implausible is "Man, they were jumping into my waders. I had to beat them off with a Louisville Slugger, and they were ripping my steel cleats to shreds. Musta hooked 120 fish in an hour." At this point the intel begins to sound very suspiciously like just plain absolute horseshit.

Absolute horseshit (A.H.) is ALWAYS secondhand information obtained from what I would consider a questionable source. A.H. would be defined as "My ex-neighbor's law partner's nephew's barber—I think his name sounds like Walsh or Wegman or something like that, told my ex-neighbor that there's this one stretch on the Upper Fork of the Little Obscurantist River about ten miles down from the dam tailout that has six-pound browns coming out of there like a vending machine, and they're all over this one fly that this guy in Bozeman ties up for a few friends when he's really pasted."

Now, let's examine that passage. First off, the name of the guy is ill-recalled and fuzzy-sounding. Walsh? Wegman? Who the heck are Walsh and/or Wegman? Or is it Welch and Weiglemann? And, there are too many layers of explanation about who the source is: if you get past three degrees of separation, you're swimming in the deep end. Who really knows who this ex-neighbor's law partner's nephew's barber really is? How large, exactly, is that so-called stretch on the Upper Fork of the Little Obscurantist? What pattern? Which shop in Bozeman? This is what I'm talking about . . . vagueness. Sounds prima facie authoritative, and yet . . . not. Too ephemeral. We just don't know, objectively, when and what to believe—or not.

Rumor is a little bit firmer than A.H.

But not much.

Rumor would be something like, "Hey, I heard that the *Existentialis crisis* mayfly is coming off on the Middle Fork of Sluggo Creek, and my ex-girlfriend's dentist nailed them. He said he caught six in an hour."

That's more credible. For example, you have two degrees of separation, there could well indeed be an *Existentialis crisis* hatch, and who among us hasn't at one time or another caught at least six trout in an hour? And you know that his ex could very well have a dentist—someone's gotta sharpen her fangs.

Now, the concept of truth is hard to define when someone is giving you some intel, but generally speaking, truth would be a first-person description from a trusted source, and what he told you would have to be on the low side of the numeric scale.

"Yeah, I ("I" is the critical pronoun) caught four (totally believable) at the Little Big Median River, and one (still credible) was fifteen (see below)."

Who would lie about a 15-inch? No one. When you're out fishing in real life, the size 15 inches fairly drips with credibility. No one says he caught a 15. He always bumps it up to 16, even if he's a person with a great track record of truth-telling, such as a friend who is a minister. Even a minister would lie about a 15-incher being "about 16."

No one gets hurt, and it's not like he was bumping a 15 up to 17, which is what some normally truthful angler would say if he had even one sip of a light beer.

Intel, in order to be fun, has to be surreptitious, like the way you would tell someone that you had certain knowledge that a senior manager was having an affair with a co-worker, and that they would meet at Jiggles on Route 34. Good intel has to be in hushed tones. It doesn't have to be verifiable, like WMD. Wait, that doesn't have to be verifiable at all. Let me rephrase that. Good intel just has to sound credible. It doesn't have to have a bunch of disclaimers like some cholesterol-lowering medication that you might see advertised on the *CBS Evening News*: "WYTAKEIT can cause flatulence, hallucinations, Pretraumatic Ideopathic Sneezing Disorder, Distended Cranium Syndrome, and should not be taken while operating even light machinery such as a weed whacker, while sitting in a missile silo waiting for launch order confirmation,

or petting cats weighing under 14 pounds." Good intel can just be taken at face value. It's not a political advertisement.

Intel should be verbally shared, and anything you read in an e-mail should be immediately discounted, because you know how people can overreact in an e-mail. Handwritten intel, preferably on cocktail napkins or the backs of keno forms in bars, or, even better, menus, have a lot of credibility. Shared spontaneous intel usually stems from some camaraderie, usually accompanied by two or more drinks. Maps accompanying intel are even more useful, because then you have the intel passer on paper, in writing, sharing some tidbit, and if it's wrong, you can sue. And God knows there's a lawyer around who fly fishes who would be more than happy to help.

Once you have received the intel, you have to make a basic decision: do I act? Do I keep it to myself? If you have a high confidence level, once you've sorted it all out, you can then go to the spot in question and try it yourself. You'll usually find it was better a few weeks ago, or that it was just okay, and not Nirvana. The info could even be months, if not years, old; the creek could have shifted, trout could have packed up and moved, or the descending hordes could well have nailed it weeks before you even got the word.

Intel sometimes doesn't pan out. One of the worst things that can happen to you as a fly fisherman is hearing a guide say, "Hey, we got 36 yesterday, and they were nailing egg patterns. Total no-brainer. It was totally ridiculous." That's when you know you're dead before you hit the ground—the intel can also raise your expectations beyond the point of any rational thought or action. You drop everything, acting on whatever intel you've got, and, believe me, intel is a faith-based initiative: you just run with it and hope that God is on your side. You drive 456 miles in six hours, loading your gear into your rig without even really looking at it—hell, you don't even load it, you throw it—jump in the car or truck, haul ass until your eyes start crossing, jump out of the car, string up, tie on whatever looks semiworkable, make a throw. Make five throws— nothing. Twenty-eight throws—nothing.

When Good Intel Goes Bad, you kick yourself for believing in Santa Claus, and you vow to make sure next time that you fully vet any future intel.

But, ultimately, you won't. You want to believe. You want to think that some fourth-generation rumor is gonna pan out, that what the Guy Milling Around at The Fly Shop—he doesn't even work there, just hangs around—swore up and down was true turned out to be a canard, and you took it like a sunnie sucking down a night crawler in a farm pond, right down to your gullet.

Fish on.

Probably the most accurate intel is based on a broad spectrum of reliable sources, the cumulative weight of the evidence over years and years of trial and error, not a wisp on the wind of a whisper.

Okay?

But listen: I got some intel for you. I swear it's true. Trust me. Take it to the bank. Use it or lose it.

Trout like worms.

FLY FISHING IN THE MEDIA

I am pretty embarrassed to admit that I used to watch a lot of television in the 1960s and 1970s, which wasn't like television is today. For example, they only had four channels: The Walter Cronkite Channel, the NBC Game of the Week Channel, the One No One Ever Watched Channel, and the Sesame Street Channel. As far back as I can remember, which was when a lot of my neighbors and even my very own family owned cars with fins on them (like trout!), the electronic media (which we didn't call it then, we used the term "TV") had very little fly-fishing content.

There was this great show on "TV," as we called it, called *The American Sportsman,* which was on the One Channel No One Ever Watched, which was also known as ABC. Interestingly, I used to contribute artwork to ABC News (*Nightline*) back when it wasn't ridiculous. It had Howard K. Smith, Ted Koppel, and Peter Jennings on it delivering what were then known as "News Broadcasts." In any event, the star of *The American Sportsman* was Curt Gowdy, who was also the play-by-play commentator on NBC's *Game of the Week*. I have no idea why Curt Gowdy was on two different television networks, but it was a simpler time. You know, Vietnam, Watergate, assassinations . . . a more innocent era.

The American Sportsman was mostly about shooting moose and elk with really big rifles, and they actually showed the dead animals getting shot. Today, of course, this would bring a class-action lawsuit on behalf of the creators of most video games as a violence copyright infringement. But in the naive 1960s and 1970s (vietnamwatergateassassinations), a program featuring majestic animals being shot was considered high entertainment. And, on occasion, *The American Sportsman* would have some fishing in it as well. I recall a lot of the shows being about massive salmon being gaffed in rivers, where the fishermen competed with grizzly bears for the fish. You haven't experienced real entertainment until you've seen a washed-up baseball player nail a nice salmon with his chaw-filled mouth. Then one of The American Sportsmen who guested on the show with Curt Gowdy (they always seemed to be movie stars, war heroes, and major sports stars of the 1940s) would shoot the grizzly bear with yet another large-caliber rifle, thus adding even more outdoor entertainment value.

But fly fishermen?

Hmm. Let me think.

If there were any on that show, I don't remember them. There may well have been some fly fishing on *The American Sportsman,* and I wasn't paying attention, but what I think is that fly fishing just doesn't have the television production value of marlin fishing. I think there was a lot of marlin fishing on *The American Sportsman.* Marlin fishing is indeed really cool, if your idea of a good time is developing abdominal muscle tears while reeling in your fish, followed by the very real possibility that your fish could decapitate you. And don't get me started on shark fishing. You need 4X at least for those things.

Bass fishermen get all the air time now. I need not go into my usual tiresome bass fishing versus trout fishing rant, but bass fishermen now have arenas with thousands of people screaming when they weigh a three-pound fish. That, to me, is like putting two freshman JV football teams on *Monday Night Football*. There is no question whatsoever that metal-flake-painted military-style boats with .50-caliber Bass Guns, lures that look like they could be manufactured by Tiffany, and badge-covered jumpsuits really put fly fishermen at a visual disadvantage. Fly fishermen do not enjoy the same level of name ID.

When I was a kid, the electronic media portrayal of the fly fisherman was something like this:

He's older, is wearing a red plaid shirt, and dons a crush cap with flies stuck in them. He smokes a pipe. He smells like Fulton's Fish Market. He lives by himself at the end of a road in an old Airstream. He has a beard that has nicotine-stained whiskers. He has a flask in his tattered vest. He hasn't taken a bath, except when he falls into a riffle. He keeps pretty much to himself, occasionally stumbling into town to buy more Yukon Jack. He drives a 1967 International Harvester truck with a thrown piston rod. He eats jerky he made himself. He used to be some sort of assistant professor at a small state university. He has two ex-wives, one of whom left him for a guy who ran a DeLorean dealership. The other one tried to kill him after one too many rambling conversations about "the goddam masking hatch." She missed and wasn't charged. He sleeps in a sleeping bag. There are various broken-down pieces of unidentifiable rusted machinery surrounding his trailer. He frequents a tavern called the Reelin-M Inn, and has been flirting with the bar waitress who is 24 years his junior. His teeth look like Indian corn.

No, wait. That's me.

Okay, it isn't me, but you know the type, and that's how the media treats him: an old coot with a very good double-haul.

If you see a fly fisherman on TV now, he is more likely to be in his early thirties and appear to be a weekend sports anchor in a medium-size market. He has an endorsement deal with Patagonia. He is presentable, noncontroversial, and Really Enthusiastic: "MAN! Those chironomids are *amazing*!"

I have seen a married couple host a fly-fishing show; that has got to be a marriage made in heaven.

"HONEY? HAVE YOU SEEN MY BOX OF BLUE WING OLIVES?"

"WHAT AM I, YOUR &*#?!! GUIDE? GO FIND THEM YOURSELF!"

And what about the ancient but still durable institution of radio?

I have always hoped there would be a really contentious fly-fishing radio call-in program, since tensions can run very high in any given angling conversation. I have seen grown men rip into each other like the Sharks and the Jets over Mustad versus Tiemco hooks. Radio now encourages this sort of thing; when I was growing up, radio was pretty tame. Call-in shows that I can recall listening to in Minnesota on WCCO-AM ("The Good Neighbor to the Great Northwest"—a slogan sure to build ratings with those seeking on-air conflict) were often about pesticides or some fascinating new development in forestry. Sometimes they would stray into animal husbandry on a really wild day. I believe there were also sometimes discussions about the Vikings and the Twins that bordered on opinions, but mostly it was soybean chat. Today, that just doesn't cut it.

LOUD HOST: My friends, once again the so-called elitist Mainstream Angling Media is telling you that they know what's best for

you. They think you're stupid. They don't want you to know that there are—*right now!*—secret government plans to take over the nation's trout rivers and make you fish barbless and take away your right to PowerBait. They're gonna come after your spinning rods and make you fish with Japanese hooks and you're not gonna be able to even eat anything you catch.

CALLER: Well, sir, you got a real point there, but that's not all they want . . . I heard they're gonna make us all fish with dry flies, and them things are small. Have you ever tried to tie one of them babies? You can just kiss your swivels and your Ford Fenders good-bye.

LOUD HOST: Oh, you haven't scratched the surface of what the Big Natural Resource Dictators' real agenda is . . . they want you to throw everything back, wear pastel, color-coordinated natural-fiber clothes, and make you go to a foreign country like Alaska to catch real fish.

I think fly-fishing discussion on the radio is probably better suited to NPR, where they would have a show called *Pale Morning Edition, All Zingers Considered,* or *World, Have Your Sage,* and there would be lots of high-minded chat.

NPR FLY-FISHING SHOW HOST: Recent developments in Zimbabwe have State Department analysts searching for new ways to implement a set of recommendations made earlier this month by the International Monetary Fund.

CALLER: I thought this was a fly-fishing show.

In Portland, there used to be outdoor segments on the news, but, again, there was very little fly-fishing coverage. It was always all about the salmon. I don't blame the local TV news directors for this. Salmon are big, salmon are taken from big boats, and salmon are things people like to eat. I have never, ever, seen a local TV news segment on how great the caddis hatch is this year. It's simply not as photogenic as a 30-pound salmon being gaffed. There is never any gaffing when you bring in a 10-incher.

The banter between the anchors is always pretty predictable if they do a fishing segment:

"Wow, Cyndi! That is one BIG fish! That would really smear up your Armani and wreck your manicure!"

"You said it, Ted! And we wouldn't want to get entrails on that $80 haircut you just got! Now let's go live to that Pie-Eating Contest in Forest Grove, where ActionCentralNews12 reporter Trish Tranh is reporting that . . . "

Blah blah blah. No trout segments.

I have heard a couple of fishing call-in shows. I was on a show hosted by Strayhorn Spadewater, and I am sure that the racial implications of his name were not lost on his audience. I don't think he's on the air anymore. I have never waited longer for a call, but finally one came in. You can imagine how long you could wait for a call with someone who writes fly-fishing humor. I think the caller wanted to know what the funniest nymph was. You tell me. The wacky Leadwing Coachman? The rollicking Copper John? It made me question everything.

As our media become more and more fragmented, I suppose blogs will pick up the slack line, and we can get out our fly-fishing jollies that way. People tell me fly fishing is shrinking as a sport, and my first reaction is, well, more water for us, I guess.

But I will tell you that I am thinking about taking up marlin fishing just as soon as I get my abs in shape.

What size tippet should I go with?

HE SAYS HE
CAUGHT
FOUR SCORE
AND SEVEN...

FLY FISHING THROUGH HISTORY

In 1609, a man named Izaak Walton ran out of worms. Or, more specifically, he was kind of a neatnik and decided that touching worms was "untoward and an unsightlye lugubrious travestie, a repellente practyce more suited to the anglynge of Bass." So he stopped touching worms and found a long piece of horsetail, tied it to the end of an "anglyngingeingynge switche," and then fashioned the first fly out of some thread from his chenille suit— nice!—into something that looked like a nightcrawler. He called it a "San Juan Worm."

Walton cast the fly into his home river and waited. He made another cast and waited some more. Still another. Finally, after 256,902 casts, in 1632, he hooked a branch.

But it was a start.

In 1654, Walton hooked his first trout.

In 1658, he landed one.

Fly fishing was born.

Walton then decided to open up a small fly shop in London, and called it "Ye Fishless Squire," and charged astronomical amounts of money for the equipment. Thousands of other landed Englishmen who also didn't want to touch worms patronized the shop, and Walton then started another shop called "Dan Bailey's Fly Shop." No one today is sure who "Dan Bailey" is, but some speculate he may have been the discoverer of Montana.

By 1772, six fly fishermen from the colonies—Thomas Jefferson, George Washington, Alexander Hamilton, John Adams, James Madison, and Theodore Gordon—were hanging around their local fly shop in Philadelphia and got to talking. All of the fly fishermen decided that the British Crown was too oppressive, and unfairly levied taxes on rooster feathers and bamboo, and so they decided to revolt. Everyone was totally on board but Theodore Gordon, who had to make a fly-fishing magazine deadline. In 1773, the six fly fishermen were very angry because there were no decent-size trout in Boston Harbor, so they threw a bunch of tea off of a ship in protest, plus they were really drunk on grog.

By 1776, all of the guys met at Independence Hall and signed a document calling for lower fly-tying-material taxes and bloody revolution, except for Theodore Gordon—who was doing really well on the Beaverkill River and told the rest that he'd catch up with them later because the Hendricksons were coming off nicely.

Having won the Revolutionary War, the guys all decided that America was truly the land of the free fly fisherman. Oddly, it had also become the instant preserve of retro Anglophile fly anglers who simply couldn't abide the notion of anything American. So the British economy was rescued from the sales of Hardy reels and other pieces of equipment that were engineered as well as the typical Triumph Spitfire. There were a lot of transmission and electrical problems with the British fly gear, but the new United States of America was a willing customer.

As the western expansion headed, well, westward, fly fishing grew along with the U.S. Many new fly anglers came across the

Oregon Trail, but they stopped at Denver to build over 600 fly shops in a 12-square-block area. The Donner Party ran out of flies and proceeded to eat each other. Frontier towns had shoot-outs over who had the best roll cast, and many fly fishermen were confronted with the very real possibility that, in the future, each fly fisherman would have only six miles of river to himself. Meanwhile, fly-fishing magazines were invented, and Western anglers were forced to wear colorful bandanas in order to appear photogenic. Cowboy hats were still allowed, if the angler actually owned one cow or more. Those who did not were put on a rail out of town, or ridiculed mercilessly and not given any choice in the color of their bandana.

But tensions rose in the southern United States, and the southern bass fishermen became seriously annoyed that the Anglophile Eastern/Northern Elitist fly fishermen were controlling everything, so they tried to secede. No luck. Anglophile Eastern/Northern Elitist fly fishermen beat back the bass fishermen with terribly expensive cane rods and forced them to create several television programs solely devoted to men yelling "Whoooooooooooooooooo-eeeeeeeeeeee! That's a GOOD fish!" No one ever seemed to catch a bad fish. There were no fly-fishing shows or tournaments.

By the turn of the twentieth century, the second Industrial Revolution was in full swing, and two brave men in Kitty Hawk, North Carolina, dragged their mechanical contraption to the top of a windswept dune and made the first attempt at powered flight. Sadly, they, too, were drunk, and they had actually invented the bass boat. A few hours later, after the two men had made four failed attempts to fly, a couple of men from Dayton, Ohio—Orville and Wilbur Wright—came along with an actual airplane, strapped the bass boat to the underside of the plane, and dropped them off at a nearby bass lake. The two men, A. J. Foyt and Richard Petty, quickly built another bass boat and decided to have a tournament. They had a few more tournaments, and then invented NASCAR. Orville and Wilbur became quite successful, and later moved to Ketchum, Idaho, to build mansions and fly fish on Silver Creek.

Fly fishing was kind of in the doldrums at this point. The bass-boat phenomenon was sweeping the nation, the fly-fishing equipment from England was always needing to be repaired, and there was a severe floatant shortage. Fortunately, Theodore Roosevelt, who had been reelected to the presidency in 1904 on a platform of "The Full Dinner Pail and Fly Box," brought inspiration to the nation's fly-fishing community through his obviously insane fly-fishing exploits, such as using rifles on trout. Roosevelt sent several U.S. warships on a world tour to show other countries that America had the best fly fishing in the world. Previously, President McKinley had even gone so far as to start a "fake" war with Maine and Canada over brook-trout fishing, just to prove to the rest of the world—specifically, Spain—that we were *Numero Uno* (Spanish for "Jingoistic Jerks"). In that same spirit young Dick Cheney later enlisted and decided to devote the rest of his life to public service, leading to his Secret Service Code Name, "Angler."

By the 1920s, fly fishing had taken on a new popularity, thanks to the explosion of the popularity of the Model T SUV. President Warren G. Harding, an incompetent Republican alcoholic oaf, was a well-known fly fisherman who inspired a generation of Americans to take up fly fishing without any regard to resource management, and all trout in the United States were virtually wiped out in the United States by the beginning of the Great Depression. Another Republican president, Herbert Hoover, decimated a trout creek near the White House by stocking it with large hatchery rainbows. This policy led directly to the Great Depression.

But I digress.

With the advent of the New Deal, happy trout days were here again with new government "alphabet agencies," such as the National Restocking Act (NRA), the Creek Deepening Corps (CDC), and the Pale Morning Department (PMD). After World War Two, the country was retooling to build massive new fly rods with fins, so-called "hi-fi" reels, and new suburbs devoted to the raising of small fry. By the 1960s, President Kennedy called for America to spend massive amounts of tax money to put trout streams on the moon, which we did with the creation of NASA—the National Angling in Space Agency. Soon, mankind will not only have trout fishing on Mars, but plans are currently in the works to create a manned fly shop in earth orbit by 2078. The Orbital Revolving Vehicle in Space, or ORVIS, will supply our astronomically priced gear needs for decades to come.

Social revolutions swept the world of fly fishing as well. More women wanted to be as frustrated and angry as men, so they poured into the sport in record numbers. Finally, all groups were given full access to fly fishing, and they jammed one stream in New Jersey shoulder to shoulder so that everyone had equal opportunity not to catch any trout at all due to overcrowding.

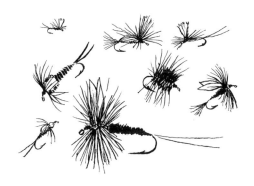

MY SWISS ARMY FLY BOX

To a ten-year-old boy seeing a Swiss Army Knife for the first time, it's like showing some starving dog a plate of T-bones. First, he stares. It has every single thing a boy could want: knives, picks, awls, screwdrivers, and scissors. In short, all boys want a portable unit that integrates everything you could put your eye out with. A perfect, simple piece of design that appeals to the basest instincts. I have what I call my Swiss Army Fly Box: it has everything you need to survive a day on the trout stream minus a cold beer and a peanut butter sandwich. My Swiss Army Fly Box is also a perfect piece of design honed after years of one &%$#* learning experience after another. I haven't painted it red and white yet, as that would be a copyright infringement, and I would not want to run into the Swiss Army unarmed. Not that I am unarmed. I just don't want any trouble, you know? I am more concerned about their lawyers, anyway.

I wish I knew more about flies. I have spent quite a bit of time studying them, and to the untrained eye, one looks about as effective as the next. Show a non-fly fisherman your fly box, and he will rightly shrug. But at some point, we have to make a call. Do I

match the hatch, go for an attractor, or just throw something out there that looks plausible?

Having started my fishing career in Minnesota, I always was attracted, like a fish, to the Rapala. If I had to pick one lure, that would be the one. You look at a Rapala and think, yeah, that will work, and when you see it in the water, it looks even better. Of course, Day-Glo spinnerbaits work great, too, and they do not represent anything I have personally experienced. They're kind of like Chernobyl Ants, which look like little lobsters/monsters/aliens, and also work really well. There are a few flies that look like they would work, and do work well. I would rank them in the following order:

1. Adams

An Adams is the baseline kind of fly you show a novice and he immediately falls in love with it. It looks like any number of common insects, which novices are well familiar with, and, hence, they believe in it at once. So it starts off with a spiritual advantage. An Adams is what you would throw out there just to see what's going on—"Attention trout: Blue Light Special on Aisle Six"—and a lot of the time, they go for it. It's almost uncanny how well the thing works. It is like a martini, a Montblanc pen, or a potato chip: you look at it and think, yeah, this will work just fine. Simple design, well executed. Nice.

2. Woolly Bugger

This fly is kind of like a Rapala in that it gives you an instant feeling of security, like a .45 pistol. A black Woolly says, I'm here, I'm on the job, the perimeter is secure, the center is going to hold, and get out of the way while I do my thing. It's nice and fuzzy, looks like about 23,673 things that float by any given trout on any given drift, and I have caught more trout with it in what seemed to be hopeless situations than any other fly. It represents everything and nothing, like a good politician.

3. Royal Wulff

God knows why it works. It imitates nothing, is hard to tie, and is more appropriately displayed on your door at Christmas than it is presented to trout. But, again, this thing works in a lot of situations, mostly because trout are so intellectually insulted that you would pitch something at them that was so . . . weird. It is one bizarre concoction, an elaborate practical joke that comes off perfectly, catches fish as intended, and yet draws guttural moans and dramatic facial tics when a fellow angler sees you using it. "Oh, God, you're not . . . using that, are you?" This is always expressed in the precise tone of voice a wife would use when you put on a tie that simply doesn't go with the suit, or when some wine-snot acquaintance questions your oenological selection. "Yeah, I'm using it," you respond, wearily, like you have to explain something obvious to a five-year-old, like how rain happens or how an engine works. You just walk them through it: I use it because it catches fish. Any other questions?"

4. Gold-Ribbed Hare's Ear

Wanna creep someone out if he doesn't fly fish? Show him your bunny ears. It gets him every time. I mean, I have made people almost throw up when they see them. It makes me feel like some sort of war criminal, and yet you can buy a nice pair of bunny ears for five bucks. It's great entertainment value. Very non-PETA, but, for a reason known but to God, you have to use the rabbit ears or the fly is just not right. Why does the olive have a pimento? Don't ask stupid questions, it just does. You stick the size 14 hook in the vise, put on the bunny ear, wrap some gold tinsel around it, and you have created a Trout Collection Unit that cuts right to the entomological chase.

H₂OBSERVATION

O ne of the trickiest skills one must acquire in fly fishing is the ability to read and watch the water. Seeing a trout rise in a lake or on a flat stretch of water is not rocket science, or even hydrology. Any rising trout in a usual spot is fairly easy to see if the water is flat, and the light is right. What I am talking about is that tiny little flick of a hint of a droplet that indicates that a trout is on the move. When I first started fly fishing back in the 1970s, I was pretty sure that I could distinguish a bass from a carp rolling in the shallows of Lake Johanna—that was like seeing Red October break the surface in a Jacuzzi. But as I got into fly fishing more and more, I saw nothing, usually, unless there were very energetic caddis hatching.

One of my most amazing fly-fishing buddies is Jim Ramsey. He has an eye like a Norden bombsight. He can circle a quarter mile up on a canyon rim, look down the Deschutes 700 yards, and say, "Oh, there's one."

No binoculars, either.

"Right there."

"Right *where?*"

"Next to that piece of water. See? The riffle."

"The riffle? The piece of water?"

"Yeah."

Sometimes his descriptive powers make certain assumptions, but he's like trout AWACS. When I say this I mean that he's one of those fishermen who would say, for example, that he caught a really nice fish on the Crooked River "by the big rock . . . you know the one." Weirdly, I usually know which big rock he was referring to. But in terms of water observation, compared with Jim, I am flying on instruments in the fog, not quite trusting the artificial horizon, and starting to question where up and down is, and Jim is seeing two-fluid-ounce splashes seven football fields downstream.

"There's a snout."

"Where?"

"God, are you blind? It's right next to that other piece of water." He loves saying stuff like that. I am always wondering how he can break water down into pieces—but he does—and we have had this conversation almost all day when we fish together. Jim is like the guy who sees UFOs all the time, and people believe him. I believe him. Then he walks down 700 yards, puts the fly right where he asserted he saw a microscopic riseform, covers it with a fly that's half unraveled, and wham.

He comes back.

"Yeah, I got it. It was right on that foam line."

"WHAT FOAM LINE?"

"The one right off the pool there behind the rock—there. See it?"

I can see glare, reflections, sparkles, trees, clouds, rock . . . no rises.

"No. I do not see it."

I forgot to mention Jim is about 75 years old and has one working eye.

He's that good.

Of course, over the years, I have developed something of an ability to see these rises. I lied for humorous purposes. Humorists do that. But I am not anywhere near as good as Jim. It's not so much that Jim is really good at seeing rises, but that he actually knows where to look for them.

"Right there? See it? Right next to that other foam line, next to that other piece of water."

"Okay. Sure. I'm with you," I will say, thinking my contacts are getting dry or that I am in need of a seeing-eye fly-fishing dog.

One thing I am really bad at is seeing fish in the water. I mean, bad. They practically have to have neon beer signs on their dorsal in order for me to see them in the water. All I see are rocks; bronze colored, undulating, stratified igneous dolomites. No trout. If I were Captain Ahab, I'd be starving to death.

"What Great White Whale?"

"That one. On the foam line. By the other piece of water."

When I saw *Jaws*, I was not really all that impressed by the story line, because I could never see the fin. Why was everyone so scared? I saw nothing.

The weird thing is, my favorite thing to do is look at water. Any kind of water. Oceans, rivers, creeks, lakes, drainage ditches, kitchen sinks, gutters, cat bowls, Perrier, whatever. I may suffer from some sort of water autism (note that Rain Man was a water-based name), but I haven't checked it. So when my water-watching skills have been called into question by other fellow anglers, I take it personally. And yet, they're right.

To the untrained eye, seeing a trout rise is kind of like having someone look up in the night sky and be told that the Andromeda

Galaxy is right over there . . . can't you see it, idiot? I mean, you *could* see it with the naked eye, but there are a lot of stars out there, it's small, and maybe you have some astigmatism. At first, when I tried to learn how to do this, one little dimple looked the same as the next. After several years of not seeing anything other than trout the size of submarines being dropped into the water from 500 feet, one microscopic droplet still looked the same as the next.

Then one day, I started noticing. Kind of.

I would intently stare at a stretch, and see them. Rings that shouldn't be there, little snouts, quarter-inch fins, and shadows. I began to feel like Google Earth for trout.

I still haven't quite gotten there yet. But I can tell you that I am better at it now than I was 20 years ago.

Now if I could only find my reading glasses to tie on this fly.

THINGS TO DO IN
FLY FISHING WHEN IT'S DEAD

Most of the time when you're fly fishing, nothing is happening. You are not catching anything. You are not seeing rises. You are not changing flies. You are not casting. You're not even falling in, which is doing something: swimming. Swimming is doing something. You are just standing in some river, doing nothing. I find that this can be relaxing. The water is soothing, the scenery pretty, and at least you're not doing anything that would stress you out, like fly fishing.

When I am in this non-fishing fishing zone, I have lots of time to do other things.

Amateur Geology! When you live in the West, many of the rivers are surrounded by incredibly impressive geological features, such as mountains, canyons, and cliffs. Whenever I see these stunning geological features, I am reminded of the fact that humans are but an eyeblink in time, and I get kind of freaked out, when I should actually be freaking out that I forgot, once again, to bring any sort of organized boxes of midges and emergers. Geologic time pales in comparison with the amount of time you spend excavating your fly boxes for the Fly That Isn't There.

Ornithology! Bird watching is one of America's fastest grow-ing pursuits, and there are indeed plenty of birds to watch while fly fishing. In Oregon, one can often see this really big one that stands in the water (I don't know what the hell it is, I don't have the Audubon Society book with me let alone a decent knot guide), as well as others that seem to have the power of flight. There are these birds that swoop down a lot of the time when there's a hatch on, and you simply can't tell what they're eating, and that makes me even more agitated. Sometimes, a duck or goose will land right in your drift, which is spectacular, and it's always right during a great hatch and there are rises everywhere. Then the rises immediately stop, and then you can try out . . .

Hunting While Fly Fishing! Yes, it is illegal to shoot ducks and geese while they sit in the water, but look, there is nothing in any state regs I have seen about attempting to hook them with a Woolly Bugger. Nothing. Check it out.

Planning More Fly-Fishing Humor Books! I find that my mind is overflowing with brilliant fly-fishing-book ideas while I am actu-ally fly fishing. I always forget what they are when I get back to the truck, and I forget to write them down in the very expensive Mole-skine notebooks I bought specifically for the purpose of writing down brilliant fly-fishing-book ideas. Hemingway was a Moleskine user, and he got a few fishing ideas out of it. Wait, I do remember a couple of the brilliant fly-fishing book ideas I had. There was *Trout Fishing in America,* which I think is a really good title for a fly-fishing book. If anyone has come up with this one, write me and let me know. One of the other ideas I had was called *Zingers and the Art of Fly Fishing Equipment Maintenance,* which sounds really cool to me, and I bet I could get 220 pages out of the zing-ers alone, because zingers are like ferrets: intrinsically funny. Dogs are funny, too, particularly if you put them on desert islands. I also have written down *The Son of a Bitch Also Rises,* which is an existential yet humorous riff on "rising" trout with a literary nod to a writer whose name I can't remember, but I think it's in my Moleskine somewhere.

Rock Throwing! Many is the time I will simply call a halt to my fly fishing and start throwing rocks. Rock throwing is cathartic when you've put in a long, hard day of fly fishing, and you would be surprised by how many fishermen you can hit if they're standing where you want to be fishing. But let's assume there are no fishermen around, and so you just want to heave a massive boulder into a pool that isn't producing: it's still cool to see *something* happening on the surface.

Thinking about Women from 1979! I find that I can spend endless hours dissecting my failed relationships, in the privacy of my own fly-fishing trip, and derive lots of insights into my own negative behavior patterns, such as talking about fly fishing to women when they, instead, want to have you endlessly and viciously dissect the personal lives and motivations of other women approximately their age. I can also delve into my past by almost verbatim recollections of scenes from dating, like when, in 1977, I allowed myself to be beaten severely at Ping-Pong by my girlfriend's father, whom I would love to have the opportunity to slaughter at Ping-Pong now, even if he's probably 80. I'd still gloat and then slam the Ping-Pong ball down in the end zone. I have transcribed all of these conversations, and have written a novel soon to be published by someone, I am quite certain, entitled *Jack: Portrait of a Man Who Has Too Good of a Memory and Would Rather Just Forget the Whole Sorry Mess.* Oh, and it's going to be a movie (I'll bet it will, I can feel it!), starring George Clooney as me, which will make it all better, and he and I can hang out and talk about fly fishing.

Devising Alternative Methods to Catch Trout! As a cartoonist, I am an admirer of the late Rube Goldberg, the inventor of the Rube Goldberg Device. If you are under 50, you probably don't even know what a Rube Goldberg Device is, but it was an incredibly complicated cartoon structure that would perform a simple task, like pouring a cup of coffee or hooking yourself in the head with a fly. As far as I know, Rube was not a fly fisherman, but it would have been great to have him figure out a way to catch trout. Here's my idea:

(A) CAT ON LADDER KNOCKS PAINT BUCKET (B) ONTO LEVER (C), HURLING BOWLING BALL (D) INTO AIR, STRIKING PASSING AIRPLANE (E), DISLODGING ITS LANDING GEAR (F) ONTO TRAMPOLINE (G), WHICH PROPELS ANGLER (H) INTO POSITION TO MAKE DIFFICULT CAST (I), ENABLING HIM TO HOOK VERY FINICKY TROUT (J).

Pretending a Snag Is a Really Big Brown! This actually happened to me last week. I was fishing in Oregon and got a snag. I whanged ("whanged" is the precise word that your rod makes when you pull on it really hard while snagged—listen to it: WHANG) back on the rod twice—hard. I was considering how I would then break off the fly. Would I walk out into the boulder and reach down, or would I just walk backward and bust it off directly? I decided on the backward walk—the current was very strong—and then I felt that the snag was moving toward me. Oh great, I thought . . . a big branch, and it's swaying toward me. It was then that I saw the tail come out of the water. The tail was about 7 inches across, and the tail was followed by a 20-inch-plus brown (yes, I have a picture). He had been foul-hooked, so I had to reel this behemoth in backward. He was hooked on the adipose fin, and the struggle was similar to the sensation of reeling in an empty garbage can turned into the current. After four hours of watching the tail sway in the air, I finally got him in, clipped the fly, and he swam off. Usually, it isn't a big brown, however, and you just have to go back to pretending. Which sucks.

Chatting with Anglers Who Fish Too Close To You! One of my faves. As I see other guys coming uncomfortably close toward me and my fishing spot, I can't decide whether to engage in banter or swear at them. As a polite Minnesotan, I always go with the banter. Not long ago, I was fishing on a really interesting river close to the Idaho border, and this older guy comes trudging down the road toward my truck. I said, "Hey, man, what's up?" in this kind of hail-fellow-well-met-faux-breezy-frat-partyish Cool Guy voice, and he kept trudging by. No response. I am thinking, "Well, Merry Christmas to you too, pal," when he turns back to me and says, "Nothing much." I then realize he's more on the 80-ish side of the equation instead of 60, and probably is a little hard of hearing. I offered him a bottle of water, because it was quite hot. I said to him, pointedly and loudly in the way no 40-something could misunderstand, "You can fish up around the bend. My buddy and I are fishing this stretch." He stares almost uncomprehendingly, nods, and then walks down *precisely* into the spot where my buddy was going to fish. I mean, right at the head of the pool. It was like I said it to him in Latin. I am leaning more toward swearing next time; maybe I can learn some Latin profanity.

Design a New Fly! After I've pawed through the wreckage of my fly boxes when I've finished determining that The Fishing Is Officially Dead, I then start pondering new fly patterns to solve the problem. I am constantly amazed by how creative and innovative really sharp fly tiers are and the variety of materials they use. I am also stunned by the number of patterns there are. Furthermore, I am floored by how many of them NEVER WORK. They look so good: great wings, perfect colors, brilliant segmentation, and NONE OF THEM ARE WORKING. So I try to think of the one that might work, and the fly-tying material that I would use is a nymph crafted solely of C-4 plastique. I wonder how the Fish and Game guys would like that? I would call it a Green Beret, which sounds an awful lot like a fly pattern.

Then there's the . . .

Why Do I Fly Fish Internal Conversation! This is something that I do constantly, because fishing is supposed to be relaxing. I would say that it's more of a diversion than relaxation, because there are all these things to do in order to actually be successful at fly fishing. Rules must be observed, protocols followed, A then B then C = D; timing must be right, positions taken, decisions made; and then, if you've done all of those things and you've indeed caught trout, then you worry about catching another trout. It's why I sometimes enjoy what I call non-outcome–based pursuits, like hiking or biking. You throw on some shoes, and walk. No success, no failure: you walk. Then you stop. Same deal with biking. Get on, ride, stop riding. No knots, no patterns, no tippet material.

Still, nothing ultimately compares with fly fishing, because it so closely imitates life itself. Get up in the morning, put on a suit, pick out a tie, answer some e-mails, make some calls, go to lunch, make some more calls, write some stuff, answer more e-mails, go home, have a drink, and look back on the day. In fly fishing, there are no suits or e-mails, but there are in fact moral equivalents: pick out the right tie/fly, make some calls/casts, answer some e-mails/trout jumping, and go home, successful or not. They also have a drink at the end in common, which is optional, but more often than not necessary.

And then there's . . .

The Hiding from Other SUVs to Avoid the Appearance That You're in a Good Spot Game! This is a diversion I engage in regularly, and it requires a great deal of skill, even when you're not catching anything. In particular, it develops quick reflexes and large motor skills. You judge the speed of the truck and make a quick judgment about how you can hide behind some brush, sometimes even throwing your rod on the bank to evade even the appearance of fishing.

If all of these diversions fail, then I sometimes will try throwing a fly around in the water. It's something to do to kill time while you're fishing.

HOW TO TIE A FLY

I'm not much of a fly tier. I can do it—my friend calls it "ham and eggs tying"—and I tie some cool flies that I can't buy in a fly shop, but other than that, I would no more sit down and tie a dozen hopper patterns than I would do something absolutely insane, like build a rod. A friend at *The Oregonian* often says that he's going to become a crazy old guy who's building a robot in his garage, and that's about what rod building is to me—the mark of someone who has completely gone around the bend.

I have read a lot of fly-tying instruction books, and some of them are pretty good. But I have not as yet seen a fly-tying book that honestly breaks the process down, step-by-step, and shows you—honestly—how to do it in a way that truly reflects what you need to know. So I provide here a basic, building-blocks guide to tying a fly.

1. Select a hook. I like to tie small flies, so I like to use a hook that I can't really see, like a 20.

2. Drop the hook into the carpet and hope you don't step on it.

3. Get another hook.

4. Put the hook in the vise. Make sure you prick your thumb when inserting the hook into the jaws, otherwise you won't have enough blood to hold the fly together.

5. Carefully wrap size 8/0 black thread around the hook shank. Take care to overwrap the hook shank so that the profile of the fly is way too fat.

6. Examine your materials and organize them carefully.

7. Sneeze.

8. Reexamine materials and reorganize them carefully. Let's try a simple pattern, like an Adams.

9. Take the tail materials (I can't remember what they are, and I can't find my tying guide, anyway). Brown hackle barbs, I think.

10. Take the brown hackle barbs off the hackle, and wrap the thread around the bend of the hook.

11. They should be sticking out .00000009 microns.

12. Switch reading glasses, again.

13. Switch reading glasses, again.

14. Switch reading glasses, again.

15. That's better.

16. Okay, get the dubbing material and rub wax all over the thread. Too much wax will make the fly body even fatter, so just screw the wax.

17. Carefully spin the gray dubbing material around the thread until it gets too twisty and the bobbin spins wildly. Six thousand rpms should work.

18. Now wrap the dubbing material around the hook shank, all the way up to the hook eye. The rear part of the fly will be fatter, even if you don't want it to be. Try squashing that fatter part down between your bleeding thumb and index finger. Good luck.

19. More blood.

20. Good.

21. Now, for the fun part. You need to tie in the wings and wrap the hackle. Clip the wings from the ends of two too-large grizzly hackle feathers.

22. Tie on the wings.

23. No, this way.

24. For the love of Pete. Please.

25. They have to be like this.

26. No, they need to be at a 45-degree angle and uprightish. Like this.

27. NO, DUMBASS. LIKE THAT.

28. Close enough.

29. Okay, now tie in your hackle. It should be grizzly and brown.

30. Get out your hackle guide to make sure that, again, they are simply too long. You will need to have the profile of the fly way too fluffy to be natural, so be careful. You can lightly trim them later in the process to assure maximum unnaturalness.

31. Now wrap the hackle around and through the wings.

32. Okay, now you have mashed the wings in a completely weird and useless position. Take your bloody thumb and forefinger and readjust them.

33. Oops. You don't need that second wing, anyway. Don't even bother to get on the floor to find it. Keep wrapping.

34. Now tie off the hackle, making sure that you can't tie off the head without having those little points sticking out.

35. Wrap even more thread around the head of the fly. More. MORE THREAD.

36. Now you can't see the points at all, but the head now looks like The World's Largest Ball of String Roadside Attraction in Fromage, Wisconsin.

37. Whatever.

38. Now do a whip finish. Take your whip finisher and get the little wire thing over the thread, rotate it, hold it up perpendicular to the shank of the hook, turn it again, rotate, twist, twist again, drop, loop, hook, and then GENTLY break the thread.

39. Good. Now, as fast as you can before the fly unravels (usually instantaneously, but sometimes you get a break and it will hold for ten seconds, just before you can get the new thread on), tie on even more thread.

40. Forget the whip finisher. Use the hollow thingee needle device.

41. FASTER.

42. Okay, now open the bottle of head cement and inhale.

43. Kidding.

44. Get the needle and dip it in the bottle.

45. Put one to eight drops of head cement on the head of the fly.

46. Compulsively stick the dubbing needle into the hook eye so it doesn't get filled in with cement. No matter how many times you do this, it will magically in-fill when you take the fly to the stream and attempt to put your tippet material through.

47. Now trim the thread.

48. You must have accidentally cut the thread, again.

49. Never mind.

50. Go to fly shop and buy a dozen Adams.

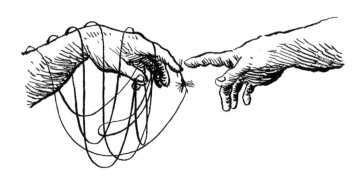

DEXTERITY

I have had many would-be and current fly fishermen assert to me that they're all thumbs, and that they simply do not have as much physical coordination as they would like in order to successfully execute their chosen hobby. And, really, who does?

I mean, I have a lot of small motor control, for a guy. I'm an artist (or, if you want to get all snide and technical about it, a cartoonist), so I operate on a fairly high dexterity level, at least from the second knuckle down. I wouldn't say I was the greatest athlete, by any stretch. I was a good baseball player, considering I weighed 140 pounds, and I am still quite good at throwing a football, considering I have four working fingers on my right hand. I broke my pinky finger playing football in 1970, and it is rather atrophied now. When I took piano lessons as an adult, my teacher told me I was never going to be a concert pianist. True, but that doesn't mean that I can't still enjoy playing the piano. The same thing goes for fly fishing: you don't have to be all that good at it to enjoy it. There are lots of things I am not very good at that I really enjoy, which I am not going to go into here.

Several aspects of fly fishing do require a great deal of dexterity: fly tying (almost impossible), rod building (absolutely impossible), knot tying (you really only need to know how to tie three knots, one of which I always have to look up), and casting (it's more time-consuming to master than difficult, like college). Let's break them down.

Fly Tying

No one expects you to be able to tie flies. Tying flies is an art form that is almost completely reliant on feel rather than any other skill, but you can always buy flies. Fly purchasing requires no dexterity whatsoever, except for the ability not to sneeze into the little plastic cup they give you at the fly shop to collect them prior to purchase. That's hard. Frankly, I feel stupid buying flies, because they're so small ("That'll be $189 for 60 small pieces of bent wire and a microscopic amount of animal fur and feathers, please"), and I know I can tie most of them myself. I just don't have the time or the inclination to do so. I never, for example, tie Royal Wulffs and Royal Coachmans. They are a royal pain to tie, and it takes about 45 minutes just to lay out all the materials. Plus, for the Coachmans you have to buy golden pheasant tippets, which are about as expensive as weapons-grade plutonium per ounce. So I just bag those. I also do not tie grasshopper patterns, even though they're very cool. I ran into some guy at the fly shop not long ago, and he was an "art fly tier." I had never heard of this. Then he showed me the very realistic-looking tarantula he had tied up. It was amazing. It looked just like a tarantula, although I have never experienced a tarantula hatch.

I would not tie my own tarantulas, either.

I tie about ten patterns that I can't seem to find with regularity in fly shops: a Deer Hair Spider Emerger; something called a Little Black Stone, which is something my buddy Jim made up; a certain type of March Brown for the Deschutes; a Purple Bodied Adams; an Adams with a Microfibett tail; and a couple of nymphs that seem to be indigenous to another river I usually fish. Other than that, I am not going to stay up late at night tying Humpies. I have other priorities, like Dick Cheney. Of course, his Secret Service Code Name was Angler. What a waste of a great Secret Service Code Name. Mine would probably be Tangler.

Honestly, my dexterity in terms of fly tying isn't all that great, either. I would say I am a kind of B minus fly tier, which is mostly good enough. My flies seem to work, if the heads are a little sloppy, the bodies are lumpy, and the hackle is almost invariably out of proportion. I know some really great fly tiers—Randall Kaufmann comes immediately to mind—and I have talked to or corresponded with a few others—Skip Morris would be another. He's outstanding. I would bet that he and Randall Kaufmann would be great microsurgeons, and I know there's big money to be made in microsurgery. Maybe one of them could fix my pinky so I could go back to my nascent career as a concert pianist.

When I'm tying flies, I just kind of go for It's Okay, It'll Work not Holy Cow, That's a Work of Art. I tend to get kind of ADD when tying; I budget about ten minutes per fly, and if I have to spend more time than that, I just get frustrated and buy them. My fingers are pretty long and thin, and so that makes for better fly-tying implements than short and stumpy. But I still glob head cement all over the place, I frequently accidentally cut the thread right when I am tying off the head of a fly, and I just cannot seem to get wings right. That's okay. As a good friend of mine once said while we were building a play structure with about 300 other people, "Don't worry about it—it's not brain surgery." He was actually a trauma surgeon, so that remark concerned me. But, hey, fly tying isn't rocket science, either. Or, to put it yet another way, another good friend of mine—a best-selling author and critic who doesn't fly fish—"You know, for a rocket scientist, you're no brain surgeon." My apologies to rocket scientists and brain surgeons, all of whom would probably make really good fly tiers.

Rod Building

No sane person would ever build a fly rod. No one. Sorry. If you tell someone that you're going to build a fly rod, you might as well just tell them that it is your intention to re-create the Apollo moon program in your toolshed using nothing but things available at Home Depot. I've tried that, and Home Depot just doesn't have the best selection of liquid oxygen. Rod building requires more than dexterity; it requires clinical monomania, which has nothing to do with dexterity, unless you are trying to get the straps adjusted exactly right on your straitjacket. There are actually people in the United States, right now, who are cutting and planing bamboo strips just *so*, in order to create cane rods. They glue the strips together. This requires all sorts of special epoxies, resins, and other completely foul-smelling sticky goos, which they have to breathe in for hours. Oh, I get it now. Never mind. They're addicted to inhalants.

Totally *whack*.

Then they do the wrappings on the guides. It takes hours and hours, and is so unbelievably easy to mess up that rewiring a Boeing 777 is comparative child's play. Following the 34 hours it takes to wrap six or eight line guides, then they have to do all the sealing with the stuff they get high on, and it can't be lumpy. It has to be perfectly uniform. Not even a Fabergé egg maker could do

it right. If I were a Fabergé egg maker, it would probably end up scrambled.

Knot Tying

Knot tying is another potential bugaboo for many anglers. While potentially superficially vexing, tying a knot quickly is more about not cracking under pressure than actually executing the knot itself. One friend, who is well documented in this and other books of mine actually once said to me: "There are two things I don't like about you: you make too many false casts, and you don't nip the tippet material off close enough to the knot." Yes, he was serious. *He said this, and he meant it.* And, yes, I do false cast too much, and I am sure that, on many occasions, I do not nip the tippet material close enough to the knot. That's just a wacky side of me that only very close friends know about. There are a lot of more irritating things about me, and not just in fly fishing. Don't get me started on my ability to survive, day after day, only on Raisin Bran, CLIF Bars, orange-flavored cranberries, tuna fish sandwiches, and Cool Ranch Doritos. Every day. I told you fly fishermen are weird.

Once you master the ability to do whatever knot it is that you need to tie tippet material together, you're in. Yet another buddy seems to spend geological spans of time tying on flies and tying tippet material. I have to stifle the impulse to go over to him and do it for him. But, sometimes, when I have caught fish and he hasn't, I have actually done this, which is something one 48-year-old guy should not take it upon himself to do for another 55-year-old guy. This other friend of mine from college used to have the same problem. Great guy, but very much like me: you want to keep the show rolling, it's hard to watch the glacial slowness of a friend, so you get a little dictatorial. He used to say to his younger brother (a new driver), when he was frustrated with him and was in a hurry, "Put the key in the ignition. Turn it to the right." And so on.

Yeah, he's a fishing writer.

Once you get kind of halfway decent at knot tying, you can pretty much do it without looking, which seems counterintuitive. As I get older, with my Dr. Dean Edell Rite Aid reading glasses set at -2.25, it's almost a necessity to be able to tie knots without being able to look at them. The dirty little secret of knot tying is not actually executing the knot per se, but actually getting the tippet material to go into the hook eye. That requires dexterity I didn't have at 18, let alone 48. I sometimes feel like I am trying to park an Escalade into a spot built for a Vespa, or maybe shoot a basketball into a Dixie cup from midcourt. Invariably, either I or someone in Sri Lanka has, as a kind of small practical joke, covered the eye in perfectly transparent head cement, leaving me comically attempting to jab the tippet into an invisible force field.

Casting

Does casting require any dexterity? Of all the tiny muscle skill sets listed above, casting requires the least amount of dexterity. Casting requires some weird sort of ability to feel exactly when the line is ready to go, and you could explain it to someone 78 billion times and they still couldn't do it.

"Look, you don't cast the fly. No, seriously. You cast the line. It's not like regular spin-casting, where, you know, you can actually catch fish."

You just have to be innately aware of when that moment is. Too much juice on the cast, and you get the whip crack. Too little and you get the wet noodle effect. I know that I am a serviceable caster, but I am also too fast, so my Casting Fascist friend tells me. I am not sure how much dexterity is involved, but the difference between a good caster and a great caster is really quite dramatic, if you know what to look for. In Idaho, this Casting Fascist friend once put a fly underneath a cutbank about 18 inches deep, maybe 2 feet up from a working Large Honker, fish takes the fly, bada bing.

That's a great cast. That's what you need to do in all this: catch that fish.

We lose sight of that sometimes. It's not really about dexterity.

Ultimately, there are many anglers fully enjoying fly fishing without having any dexterity whatsoever—why should you be any different? Saying that you need to be dexterous in order to enjoy fly fishing is kind of like saying you have to be a wine shop owner in order to enjoy a glass of wine, or turn in a 4:30 mile in order to be a jogger. I have found that my own dexterity in fly fishing gives me a false sense of confidence, anyway.

Besides, how dexterous do you have to be, anyway?

Last time I checked, trout don't have opposable thumbs.

ARE ANGLERS REALLY PATIENT?

Acommon misperception about fly fishermen is that they're patient. Hunters, on the other hand, are very patient. They sit for hours and hours in freezing duck blinds, snow-covered deer stands, sopping wet reeds, putrid muck, superheated or frozen rocks, or do whatever else they have to do in order to conceal themselves. If they are not sitting motionless for days waiting for some deer to come up within 300 yards, or hoping for some microscopic bird to fly within radar range, they are actively stalking them for miles in conditions that would put the average angler or letter carrier to utter shame. On the other hand, I know quite a few fishermen who will not go fishing if it's below 70 degrees. Hunters will remain completely silent, breathing only when absolutely necessary. Fly fishermen will chat endlessly while fishing (or not), and will only move stealthily when so ordered by a guide they're paying $300 per day. My experience with fly fishermen is not only are they not patient, they tend to be about as patient as the average Camp Lejuene master sergeant. Yesterday is not soon enough for the typical angler.

This alleged patience is only on display with bait fishermen, who willingly stare for hours at a bobber. This is something that I actually enjoy doing, and did endlessly in Minnesota. Bobber-staring (or bait fishing) is kind of soothing, particularly if you are sitting in a lawn chair. If someone could figure out a way to integrate lawn chairs into fly fishing, I guarantee you that fly fishing would become much more popular than it is now. For example, you have to stand up all the time in fly fishing. Standing up is stressful. Sitting in a lawn chair and staring is not.

Naturally, fly-fishing snobs will argue that dry-fly fishing requires patience. Indeed, dry-fly fishing is really only a fancy way of bobber fishing, and everybody knows it. Same principle sans the red-and-white plastic: hope that baby goes under. I won't even get into indicator fishing, because any intellectually honest fly fisherman knows that's bobber fishing. Does dry-fly fishing require patience? Well, let's put it this way: I hear way more dry-fly fishermen say things like, "Goddamn it!" than I have ever heard bait fishermen say. I have been with two other guys in the same drift, and we're all saying "Goddamn it!" all the time, like we're in an echo chamber. Maybe once in a great while, a bait fisherman will say that right when he has to get out of the lawn chair to bend over and pull the fish out the water, but mostly dry-fly anglers take oaths about every two minutes or so. I know I do. We say that either audibly, or, more often, under our breath, which you may think doesn't count, but it does. Same stress level. What are the circumstances a dry-fly angler would say, "Goddamn it!" and why?

1. Missing a strike.
2. Breaking the fly off on a strike.
3. Thinking that you are going to get a strike when you put the fly right over the trout, and nothing happens.

4. When you have to change leaders.

5. When you have to change tippets.

6. Breaking off a fish.

Where is the patience in that? If fly fishermen are so patient, why the swearing? Sometimes, to vary the routine, dry-fly fishermen will say, "Goddamn it" if they're particularly upset about something, like having to tie an Albright knot.

I can also report accurately that fly fishermen are not at all patient when it comes to gear. In fact, most fly fishermen are changing their gear all the time. *All the time.* Bait guys never change their gear. I still have the same Garcia Mitchell 300 reel I had from 1972, and it works just fine. I don't care. Monofilament winds around, handle turns—beautiful. Fiberglass rod, same deal. I'm like, whatever. You never hear bait guys talking about the "sensitivity" of their rod. Works for me. I have the same stinking tackle box I got in 1979, and I never even bothered to replace it after all the plastic worms melted the ABS plastic, or whatever it's called. I use 35-year-old lures. It's not like the fish care if the Bass-Oreno is not exactly perfect. On the other hand, fly guys are constantly looking for ways to improve, upgrade, and get that tiny strategic edge that they need to catch a fish. If that insatiable quest to continually get new gear is an indication of how patient fly fishermen are, then I have a new word to describe them: golfers.

Another indication of the patience of the average fly fisherman: despair.

I run into very few despairing bait fishermen. I feel like I am a crisis counselor to at least two fly fishermen I know.

"Look, Dave . . . it's not the end of the world. You missed some strikes. You couldn't figure out the hatch. Good people miss strikes and misread the hatch all the time . . . it's okay."

"But . . . but . . . I . . . *failed.*"

Bait fishermen never need interventions. They just kind of sit there, staring at the bobber, ever optimistic that sometime the bobber will go down, and, if it doesn't . . . cool. They'll go dig up a dozen more night crawlers tomorrow. Who cares? It's only fishing. Fly fishermen are the most neurotic class in all of American outdoor sports. They feel judged all the time, and this translates into a kind of weird lack of patience that only superachievers have. There are no fly fishermen who I know would fall into the category of "slacker."

Okay, one guy.

But almost all of the others are in highly demanding professions or would easily qualify as "not patient" in any sort of objective trial. What fly fishermen are really good at is creating the illusion of patience.

This illusion of patience is best applied with non-fishermen. "Oh," they will say at a cocktail party when they hear you fly fish, "you must be *patient!*" That is perhaps the most obvious thing you could say to a fly fisherman, with the exception of "Oh, why don't you *eat* them?" Once they say, "You must be patient," you usually respond with a small chuckle, pretend you are puffing on a pipe, and say something along the lines of "Yes, I am terribly patient. I am so patient about fly fishing that I just got a ninth $685 fly rod in order to quickly and efficiently get that fly into the water that much faster. Mr. Patient. That's me. Now get the hell out of the way of the canapés."

Another demonstrable test of the fly fisherman's general lack of patience is driving. Most fly fishermen are speeders—the very definition of lack of patience. Any fly fisherman, particularly a Western fly fisherman, has a number of serious speeding tickets. I myself have received three specifically related to fly fishing. I have gotten one warning. I have been in the car as a passenger when one citation was issued, and one warning. I'm not proud if it or anything, and I am much more careful now, mostly because speeding requires more attention than not speeding at age 48. One time, a friend of mine was driving like a bat out of hell in what I was pretty sure was Wasco County, Oregon, a lightly populated area where sagebrush and snakes are the dominant life forms. We were trying to get to the Deschutes River, I am certain, and my friend is not exactly laid back.

A Warm Springs Reservation police officer in a Jeep Cherokee followed us for a number of miles before actually pulling us over. When he did, he ambled up to the car and he stuck his head in the driver's side window.

"Do you fellas know how fast you were going?" he asked, helpfully. I am sure he just wanted to let us know that we were just under Mach 4, and maybe we should turn on the afterburners to get maximum power.

My friend said, to my amazement, "Aren't you out of your jurisdiction?"

I sat quietly, expecting to be either thrown over the hood of the car with my face pixelated, or, perhaps, the recipient of six warning shots in the forehead. I closed my eyes. I heard the theme music from COPS in my head: "Bad boys, bad boys, what you gonna do when they come for you?"

"What did you just say?" the officer asked, again, making sure that he, in fact, heard what he just heard.

"Aren't you out of your jurisdiction?" my buddy said, again, this time more slowly so that the officer had plenty of time to get his GLOCK in position.

"Sir, I am a sworn officer of the State of Oregon, and this is my jurisdiction."

"No, it isn't. We're not on the Warm Springs Reservation now. You're out of your jurisdiction."

Oh, God.

I kept thinking, one, this is gonna hurt, and two, I do not have enough money for a lawyer right now.

After a few more go-rounds with the officer, for some astonishing reason, the guy let us go. I vastly underestimated the patience of my friend. Maybe he was just more patient than I had given him credit for, as a fly fisherman. I guess he *was* out of jurisdiction. This is why I admire this friend so much. He shows selective patience.

Fly fishermen also show a stunning lack of patience in fishing conversations with fellow anglers. In a normal, ideal, typical conversation, two people will amiably exchange anecdotes about whatever is going on in their lives, thoughtfully providing the other participant with the time to respond in kind. Fly fishermen are constantly and continually cutting each other off, trying to one-up the other on whatever permutation of angling they happen to be conversing about.

"I caught a 19-incher on a size 22 with 7X, and I had to drive 590 miles while it was snowing like . . . "

"Oh, I caught a 23 on a 28 with 8X, and I had to drive 1,320 miles during a 7.4 magnitude . . . "

"Oh, really? Well, I caught a 29 on a 38 with 9X, and I had to fly the space shuttle *Endeavour* 145,000 miles during a tactical nuclear . . . "

"Huh. Well, I caught a . . . "

I suppose that patience is a virtue, but it is not a virtue shared by fly fishermen. Another thing is that fly fishermen tend to be very impatient when it comes to lots of other aspects of the pursuit. They are impatient with fly selection. If one fly isn't working, boom. That fly is gone and another fly takes its place. If a fly angler isn't happy with where he's standing in a river, he moves to another spot in the river. If a fly angler isn't happy with the river he's fishing in, he goes to another river.

Some of the most searing moments of impatience that I have ever experienced are with other fly fishermen. I have had my casting critiqued, without prompting, multiple times with multiple fishing friends. I have critiqued other fishing friends' fly selection, and yet I would never say anything about their tie, decorating, car, kids, wife, or even their politics. Okay, maybe their tie, if it was really terrible. Would other hunters critique the way another hunter holds a gun?

Maybe. But only once.

GEAR WE DON'T USE

Iknow that fly fishermen are supposed to be gear-obsessed, and to a certain extent, most are. I am more intrigued, however, not by the fisherman who has everything, but by the fishermen who have virtually nothing. I would say that anyone, for example, who fishes with a Pflueger Medalist reel, and cannot really say precisely what kind of rod he has other than it had once belonged to his grandfather, would fall into this category. I have a friend who only fishes with flies his late father used. In fact, the one time I went fishing with this friend, his father, who had died some years before, came with us. In a can. I think it was a coffee can. In fact, we had to go back to his house and get his father's remains before we left.

I have to say that I actually enjoyed fishing with his father, who, unlike a lot of people I fished with, never complained loudly about how lousy the hatch was, or how hard the wind was blowing, or how all the trout were short-striking. When we got down to the river, the father sat in the car, didn't bum flies, and generally occupied his time politely while we flogged the water into billowing suds. As we were driving back, I found myself directly addressing the father as well. He did as well as we did—nothing.

Anyway, my friend wasn't gear-obsessed. I liked that. I would say that I am not, either; but I was, 15 years ago. I had lots of reels and spools, too many expensive rods, the cool bag from Orvis that I now use to put the overflow fly boxes from my vest in, and about 16 billion little gadgets in my vest that I never, ever used. I think I had about the normal level of gear for someone of my skill set. On the other hand, my much more skilled angling friend Jim Ramsey, whom I fished with constantly at the time, had a pretty low-end Orvis rod, a Scientific Anglers reel, and a vest that smelled. It smelled very bad. It smelled like me and the Pittsburgh Steelers after we had been fishing all day. It had this big dirt smear on it—look, it wasn't dirt, it was more like dirt, slime, fish poo, river algae, and anything else that came out of whatever orifices man and fish possess—and I actually became so physically ill when I looked at his vest that I finally, for his birthday, bought him a new one. I couldn't take it anymore. Thank God he decided to wear it, because the one he had was something out of the 14th century in terms of public health.

As I dug around my fly vest and tying chest the other day, I came upon things I never use. I do not wish to name manufacturers, because, well, that's not fair to them, because I know that other, more intelligent anglers make very good use of what these people make. I will refer generically to these things, and hope none of the manufacturers figure out what I'm referring to and issue a fatwa.

Whip Finisher

I have tried to use one once, and it seemed like it only compounded my fly-fishing dyslexia. I know it's supposed to be easy to use, but it was the turnaround phase aspect of it that left me . . . um . . . feeling almost ill when I tried it. Besides, what's the whip part all about? What is the whip? How do you finish the whip? Is the whip incomplete without the finisher? Hmm? Tell me. I know. I will get 600 e-mails from readers telling me precisely when, how, and why to use a whip finisher, and I will appreciate hearing from you all, but I am not interested. Save it. Send me some flies instead so I don't ever have to use a whip finisher. Thank you.

Bottle of That Fly-Drying Dust

I have had the same bottle of fly-drying dust for about 18 years. I have used about one-third of it. I call it Fly Sugar, because that's what it looks like. I can't imagine what the markup is on it, and I bet sugar works as well as or better than this stuff. My buddy uses it all the time, but I just false cast constantly anyway. I know I should use it. Sorry.

Those Little Sinkers from England

I bought a container of these things about 20 years ago, and I still haven't touched them. I may have put one on, once, as a kind of "Hail Mary" to get a streamer down farther, but usually these sinkers just sit quietly in my vest, drinking lime and lagers, eating bangers, and waiting for the British Empire to reassert its primacy over the Realm. They're cute and all, but I just don't use them.

The Seine

Well, when I first got this net for catching and identifying whatever was floating downstream, I pulled it out a few times and felt like an undergraduate biology student the whole time. I am sure I would be a better fisherman if I actually used it, but it just never occurs to me. I am now to the point where I can kind of tell what's going on, anyway, or I have pretty good intelligence from someone about what nymphs to put on. So this is another thing that sits in my vest, chatting up the little sinkers from England.

Stream Thermometer

I have used this a few times, like 15 years ago. The thing is, thermometers only measure what you already know: the fishing sucks because it is too cold or too hot. All knowing the water temperature is going to do is buy you 30 seconds of conversation back at camp.

"Man, the fishing really blew this morning. My thermometer said the water temperature was 36 degrees."

"No . . . really? Now help me with this ice pick."

If a thermometer could somehow measure why in God's green earth trout aren't taking my perfectly presented, well-tied, hatch-matched fly, then I might have some reason to pull it out. It doesn't. So it stays in the vest.

Classy Leather Leader Wallet

Back when I went through what many fly fishermen go through—the By God, I'm Getting Serious about Fly Fishing or Quit Moment—I bought this cool leather leader wallet. At the time, I was making my own leaders or using only hand-tied leaders made by friends (you can see why the divorce rate among fly fishermen is above average), so of course I needed to buy the requisite container (fly fishermen love containers of all kinds, and hoard them: coffee cans, cigar boxes, film canisters, small plastic boxes, Ford Explorers), so I picked up the leather leader wallet to go along with the duck fabric, leather-bottomed satchel, and the two cane rods I bought in quick succession. Now I just jam the manufactured leaders in my vest and don't really do the micro-obsessoid hand-tied leaders anymore—I have other things to obsess about, such as why I write more about fly fishing than actually fly fish.

Flexible Flashlight

This thing is like some sort of bizarre 1950s design inspired by B-grade alien movies. At twilight, when I am supposed to be using it, I just keep forgetting I have it and just mutter a lot about how I can't see. I prefer cursing the darkness rather than lighting a candle. I just kind of tie on the fly in the fading light by the Braille Method rather than, you know, becoming Man the Toolmaker. Sometimes I put a little flashlight in my mouth. Then I really look like a 1950s alien movie.

Portable Fly-Tying Kit

Yes, I actually have a portable fly-tying kit in my vest. I spent hours putting it all together, with a special emphasis on midge materials as well as enough fur and feathers to whip out a half dozen of virtually every conceivable dry pattern nature can throw at me. I have used it once, in 1993.

There was some midge hatch coming off in Idaho on the St. Joe River, and I couldn't get them to take my usual Griffith's Gnat gambit. The Griffith's Gnat is what you throw at them right before you start crying, unless, of course, you have assembled a portable fly-tying kit. What I don't like about having a portable fly-tying kit is:

A. It eliminates any and all excuses about not being able to match the hatch.

B. If your buddies find out you have a portable fly-tying kit in your vest, they will want you to tie up some flies for them, if you're not doing anything at that moment.

I have spent a decade and a half not telling my friends that I have one on me. I still have it, but, you know, I am not going to bang out five #22 chironomids just because one of my lesser-prepared comrades asks me. I have better things to do.

Like clean out my vest.

Myrtlewood Trout Call

I just blow into it, and the trout come. Apparently it emits some sort of high frequency pitch that only can be detected by trout, and the thing really works. Mine is made out of engraved myrtlewood with a scrimshaw inlay; it was hand-carved by Norwegian fishermen in the 1870s, and it's worth thousands and thousands of dollars. Very intricate. But I hardly ever use it now because I am so danged good at fly fishing.

WINTER FISHING

As I write this sentence, it is snowing outside. Having lived in the Midwest for a long time, this shouldn't surprise me, really, but in Portland, it's a major shock. When it snows three inches, all molecular motion ceases. There is live coverage from all the major freeway overpasses, it makes the front page of the paper, and people drive into things they shouldn't drive into. In the Midwest, if it snows three inches, all it means is that all the shoveling you did that morning has to be redone. It does not merit a mention on the news. It is referred to in two-point type on the weather page. Finally, what it really means is that you don't go fly fishing. At all. Ever. But you can go ice fishing if you want to.

Ice fishing, for those of you who haven't done this, can be done three ways:

1. You walk out onto the ice, chop or drill a hole into it, and stand over the hole with a very short pole and not catch anything.

2. You drive out onto the ice, chop or drill a hole into it, and then lean out of your car door with a short rod and not catch anything.

3. You drag a small plywood house out onto the ice, get terribly drunk, and completely forget why you were out there in the first place.

Once you get your head around the fact that you are sitting in the middle of a lake, in a shack, watching the Vikings, Bears, or Packers, drinking a Grain Belt, making chili, and fishing at the same time, then you have to admit that standing outside waving a fly rod in an Alberta Clipper seems somewhat less fun in comparison.

Oh, I am sure there are some maniacs who go fly fishing in the Midwest in the winter. If some guys can find moving water, they'll go. There is not a lot of moving water in the Midwest in the winter. Nor is there a lot of moving water within 1,000 miles of the Midwest in the winter. In contrast, there is some sort of available fly fishing to do year-round in Oregon. Some of it inevitably involves steelheading.

I don't want to tee off too hard on winter steelheading, as it's a state religion, but mostly it's just a miserable freezing drippy debacle. I can do that without making a 100-mile drive; I can just stand in my front yard for eight hours in January when it's 35 and raining. Same practical effect: wet, no fish. Summer steelheading at least affords one the opportunity of catching some rays, if not fish. If you complain about the weather during winter steelheading, it's a bit like volunteering for the Finnish Army and then asking to be stationed in the Bahamas. *Bonne chance.*

In any event, I have done a lot of winter fly fishing. It seems like I go more in February and March than I do the rest of the year. Fishing in the winter has a particular set of challenges and rewards, but one thing is true: not many other people are as insane as you are; hence, you get a lot of water to yourself, even in Oregon. Most serious but mentally stable fly fishermen will use the interim winter solstice to clean out vests, tie up those 133 dozen midges they've

always meant to do, oil their reels, and get reacquainted with significant others, like divorce lawyers. But once you've made that initial decision to become a winter fly fisherman, it's a road that gets covered with black ice quickly.

To deal with the very real problem of staying warm while standing in water that's 36 degrees, winter fly fishermen develop coping strategies. I have the following little tricks that always keep me toasty.

A. Neoprene burns rather well, and if you stay in water that's only knee-deep, you can keep a low smolder going on in your waders for hours.

B. Fiberglass long johns.

C. I keep a small electric heater in the back of my vest, running an extension cord into my Tahoe.

D. I spread hot maple syrup all over my torso.

If you decide that none of my hints are plausible for you, then you can use typical methods, such as warm clothing, or stuffing a Significant Other into your waders.

One of the main problems with winter angling is ice. Ice will form in your guides pretty quickly when you're fishing in subfreezing temperatures. However, once your guides are frozen, they'll stop criticizing your casting style. Now let's talk about the line guides. Ice will form quickly in those as well, and you will have to break it out or melt it with a blow torch, which I prefer.

One of the upsides of winter angling is that it is incredibly easy to keep your fly dry, as it doesn't actually hit any moving water. There's no floatant, no false casting, just a perfect upright dry fly every time. This cannot be underestimated as an advantage.

Cold, non-working fingers are usually a problem as well, and there are multiple solutions here. Breaking the fingers off will be relatively easy, and they can be stored and surgically reattached by any competent plastic surgeon. I like keeping my frozen, removed fingers in a Ziploc bag for use later. Another way to deal with frozen fingers is to just forget about using them at all, and the feeling goes out of them after about five minutes of intensive fly fishing. You'll need to monitor their color, and when they go purple, that's a good time to put them in the Ziploc. Of course, you could try to keep them warm by periodically dipping them in tempura batter, or by drinking lots of hot toddies while fishing. This will keep your fingers warm, but you will make increasingly poor fly selection decisions, and, indeed, any kind of decision at all may be questionable, like immersing your entire body to equalize the finger temperature. When you start seeing visions, that's when you should consider stopping your fishing trip and get yourself to a major medical facility. A vision would be defined as catching a fish.

Knowing when the trout has actually taken your fly is tricky when you've lost consciousness from the cold, but keep practicing! Your slowed physical response will complement the almost comically dead takes and fights you'll experience when catching trout cryogenically.

Mistaking a heavy snow squall for a cream midge hatch is a common problem in winter angling. If the midge melts on your tongue, it's probably a snowflake. If the snowflake flutters off your hand and a trout smashes it, it's probably a midge. If you squeeze the snowflake between your thumb and forefinger, and a little gray smear squeezes out, it's a midge. If the midge is really cold and crystalline, it's most likely a snowflake. If you drop a box full of them in the river because your fingers are numb, they're definitely midges.

The advantage to fly fishing in winter is that it shows commitment to your peers, which is always useful in a guy setting. Other fly fishermen are usually high-testosterone super-achieving competitive types, and they always seem to respond to gestures that indicate some sort of wild devil-may-care effort on the behalf of others. In the movie *Animal House,* which was not about fly fishing but actually illustrates quite clearly the ethos of the typical group of fly-fishing friends, there was a scene where Otter, played by Tim Matheson, says at a frat meeting, "What this calls for is a senseless, stupid gesture on somebody's part." Fly fishermen love senseless, stupid gestures, like driving astronomical distances in blizzards to make some obscure hatch that comes off for 30 minutes, dry-fly fishing in 68 mph winds, spending hours perfecting that one perfect pattern at the bench until you're cross-eyed, and standing in a river that is two degrees above being ice.

One of the silliest things I have ever purchased in fly fishing is a pair of neoprene gloves with an exposed finger. This glove works, to a certain extent, but your finger is always frozen a dark purple hue, has no extension or flexibility, and is generally unprotected from the elements. And yet, I paid $40 for the privilege of owning a pair because I am A Serious Fly Fisherman, and the number one thing that a fly fisherman loves to be thought of is Serious. The second thing he likes to be thought of is tough, as in: "I stood in the Upper Bigmouth all day during a blizzard and didn't get a bump."

Real people just think you're nuts.

THE SKINNY ON THE KINNI

Every fly fisherman I know has a boyhood stream. Mine was the Kinnikinnick, which is a small brown-trout stream that runs around the Wisconsin college town of River Falls, a delightfully named locale about an hour from the Twin Cities. Now, the Kinnikinnick is not the greatest trout stream in the world, or Wisconsin, or perhaps even within two hours of the Twin Cities, but it was where I really learned how to fly fish, or, more accurately, how not to fly fish. I caught more trout there by accident than on purpose, which is kind of the point of learning how to fly fish. Mistakes were made, as political and corporate wrongdoers say in the passive voice to mitigate wrongdoing, and I made a lot of them. But it was also the place where I caught my first brown on a fly that I tied myself, the first place where I used dry flies, and the first place I could drive to myself to catch trout. Like any first romance, I have completely magnified the larger meaning of it all, recalled things that probably never actually occurred, and generally viewed the whole experience like any self-respecting delusional humorist with a fatal streak of nostalgia would do.

The Kinnikinnick, in the mid-1970s, ran through farm pas-
tures and backyards (mostly backyards) and was maybe 30 to 60
feet wide in most places, narrower in some, wider in others, but
was easily wadable and had good overhanging tree cover and lots
of moss and boulders. The gravel was not great, as I recall, and
it had started to silt up dramatically when I went back in the late
1980s, probably due to the housing developments that had sprung
up above its banks since I had last fished there. I would fish the
stretch below the dam in town, which had a nice tailwater that I
never actually bothered to fish mostly because there were usually
kids fishing in it with worms. I cannot remember if it was designated fly fishing only at the time, but my recollection was that it
was. I do remember very clearly one day in 1980 going over to the
dam with my fishing buddy, Mark Strand, who was not the Poet
Laureate of the United States, but the real Mark Strand from the
Minnesota Daily, who was and is a truly talented fishing writer
and fisherman.

Mark Strand was also talented in hockey, and had a strong
resemblance to any given 1970s TV action hero with a mustache
and an uncanny ability to talk to regular guys while drinking beer.
I, on the other hand, was a skinny self-conscious 20-year-old with
hair that can only be described as too large. I had more zits than
whiskers. Still, we got along well. He was quippy and had several
quotable brothers who were also hockey types. It was good to be
a hockey type in Minnesota—way better than being a cartooning
type.

Mark Strand and I went on a number of fishing adventures in a
short period of time, and his parents owned this absolutely amazing island in the middle of Lake of the Woods, Canada. There was
no trout fishing, but there were lots of walleyes, muskies, small-
ies, largemouths, northerns, crappies, pumpkinseeds, bluegills, and

lake trout. One time I flew up there in a DC-3, which seems almost laughable now, but that was the regularly scheduled airline to International Falls as late as 1984, which was the last time I went up there. As the DC-3 was the workhorse plane of the Crimean War, I would probably drive there now instead.

Anyway, Mark Strand and I walked by the dam on the way down to the river (the path from town ran by it), and we encountered a boy about ten years old. Mark could see that he was concealing something.

"Catching any?" Mark asked in what could only be described as the voice brothers use to bust younger brothers' chops.

"Just one," the child said, revealing the 19-inch brown he had behind his back. The little bastard.

See? The lying in fly fishing starts almost in the womb. I am sure the kid is now a great $300/day guide—probably makes a ton telling his clients to surreptitiously tie on a night crawler to the Royal Coachman and fling it at the dam tailout.

Mark Strand and I then took off down the grassy banks; I must have been using my usual Gold Ribbed Hare's Ear, which is the Rapala of flies: it always works. I am not sure what he was using. In any event, Mark peeled off (or maybe I did), and we got separated. Really separated. I mean, I never saw him again that night. We should have communicated more effectively, but we didn't, and it was around 11 PM when I decided to head back to the truck. It was a brilliant full moon, and there was plenty of light, particularly to illuminate the beaver splash right next to the path that made me void my pants; I have never been so scared in my life. It sounded like someone had dropped a grand piano into the river from, well, a DC-3. I had that Fresh Taste of Metallic Adrenaline coursing through my mouth as I picked up my pace back to where I thought the truck was.

It wasn't where I thought it was. It was really not where I thought it was.

By this time, I was exhausted and disoriented. I had lost the trail in the dark, had no flashlight, and felt like I was stumbling around in heavy mosquitoes with no frame of reference at all. Finally, in one of my last acts of conscious thought, I made my way up a hill toward some amber lights. I found myself in one of the aforementioned suburban developments that had sprung up since the mid-1970s. I walked up to a house that still had lights on, and knocked weakly on the door.

A man answered. I explained my predicament. I was wiped out, didn't recognize where I was, and needed directions back to the park.

"What park?"

"The one by the dam."

"I'm a police officer."

"Cool. I haven't done anything illegal, I am sober, and I need help."

So he took me over in his police cruiser, after determining I was not a credible threat to person or property. My friend was sitting in the truck, as he had been so doing for several hours. He was . . . upset.

"Where the hell have you been?"

"Uh. You went ahead, I lost the trail, there was this beaver the size of a boxcar . . . "

"Get in."

He seemed less than interested in the fact that I had hooked a 13-inch brown, which was pretty big for the Kinni. In fact, it was the biggest brown I had ever caught in there. I think I was using an emerger, but it all ran together.

It reminded me of a trip I was supposed to take to the Kinni in 1976.

July was hot that year; Minnesota was undergoing a typical muggy, soupy heat wave. My mother had agreed to take me and my friend Tim over to the river, we would camp for the night, and then come back when his mother would pick us up. I walked into the living room to tell Mom we were ready to go. She was sitting in her chair, crying.

"What's the matter, Mom?"

"It's . . . it's . . . he's dead. He's dead."

"Who's dead? Did Dad die?"

"Yes."

"Oh my God. Dad is dead?" I started to cry, too.

"How did he die?"

"In a gas station in Green River, Wyoming. He hit his head on the grease rack. He had an aneurysm."

Now, at this point, I was pretty sure that my dad was not, in fact, in Green River, Wyoming. My mom meant that her dad was dead. My grandpa.

I was somewhat relieved to find this out, but only slightly. I loved my grandpa. He was moving from Salt Lake City back to Denver with my grandma. She was sitting in the car waiting for him to come back. My grandfather was of the generation where you would get out of the car and go talk to the mechanic while he filled up the car. He would carefully record his mileage in a little green book with each fill up. Grandpa had a gorgeous 1963 white Lincoln Continental hardtop with suicide doors, and I think he changed the oil every 200 miles. He walked over to the grease rack, said something (probably about gas mileage), and then collapsed. He was dead before he hit the ground.

My Uncle Hal had to drive from Salt Lake City to pick up my grandma, who was 78, waiting for her son to get her and his dead father. The night before, Grandpa had decided to sleep on the bare floor. They had an argument the night before. They always argued.

"You know, I have always loved you," Grandpa said that evening.

"You sure had a funny way of showing it," she noted correctly.

He was dead the next day. No good-byes, just got out of the car and that was it. Not the way anyone would want it to end.

So we didn't go to the Kinni that day.

I have had some wonderful days there. I remember the first trout I hooked there. I was not sure what it was supposed to feel like when I got a take. My prior trout experiences had been in big boats, trolling Helin Flatfish (my favorite was a frog pattern) in Utah's Strawberry Reservoir, and there was no question in anyone's mind that you had hooked a 17-inch cutthroat. It always took violently, almost like a small, angry child was on the end of the line, pulling and tugging insistently. I knew the trout were small—I was warned about that. What happened was, I felt a sensation that was almost electric, like I had stuck a fork into a wall socket. The trout shook off after about three seconds, but it was unmistakable: a trout had taken a fly I had presented, horribly, awkwardly, and yet it still managed to work. I had hooked a fish in the Kinni.

Later trips revealed more tricks and techniques. I once used a little green worm pattern and that pulled in a trout or two. Fishing the Kinni was more like a long hike in water, rather than fishing. I still have dreams about it, 33 years later. The houses with the long Midwestern lawns, the big flat stretch, the beautiful porches and the swing sets and the running lawn mowers and the overhanging willow trees; all of that plays out in my mindscape as the ideal now, even if the fish were small and hard to catch.

My dad and I went over there once; a friend of his at work had given him a few small gray nymphs to try, and those worked, too. I stood in one spot and pulled out a good number of fish from a cutbank while a dutiful Wisconsinite cut his grass, seemingly oblivious to my success. I recall coming down around a bend and seeing my friend Lars, who had caught a lot of fish and had put them in a baggie, I think. I had a small creel, something I never use now, and that I never, ever see anymore. Lars was an expert angler, for his age. He tied the hackleless dry flies as popularized by Swisher and Richards; and to me they still seem almost comically useless, but Lars had figured it all out. Of course, he was very smart and methodical; he's a doctor in Seattle now, and that didn't surprise me in the least bit. I am sure he doesn't baggie his fish anymore.

I always took every fish home with me. They were beautiful even in death, with their bright red spots and the buttery yellow sides. I can still remember them. I photographed them, arranged them in grass tableaus, showed them to neighbors, and then I ate them.

I will never have a better time fly fishing.

I miss the Kinni terribly, I miss the black Midwestern thunderstorm skies, I miss the humidity and the tiny rises and the tall moist grass, and I will return someday.

With a map and a flashlight.

And an ear out for beavers dropped from DC-3s.

A CAST OF THOUSANDS,
A COST OF MILLIONS

One of the main problems with deciding to start fly fishing is that you eventually have to learn how to cast. Of course, there are shortcuts involved, and almost anyone can make a 20-footer without too much trouble, but in order to really get proficient at fly fishing, you have got to be able to master the physics of casting.

That means lessons. That means studying casting, practicing casting, and looking stupid while learning how to cast. No one, particularly successful adults, wants to look stupid. Sadly, there is a long learning curve and a corollary long stupidity curve. There are enough aspects in my life where I look stupid. Shall I delineate them?

Talking to women. Hitting a driver. Attempting to explain eighth-grade math. Trying to figure out what, precisely, is wrong with the black water tank on my Airstream. Playing Ping-Pong with my kids. Playing ANY video game with my kids. And so on.

But casting is something I can now do at least halfway decently, and it has only taken me since the Nixon Administration to get a handle on it. Not that I really have all that great of a handle on it.

I don't. Sometimes when I'm around a really great caster, I realize that I am kind of slinging hash while he's whipping up a nice *coq au vin*. I can recall early efforts by Well-Meaning Others while I would make these horrendous throws, and the patient I'm-Talking-to-a-Three-Year-Old voice I would hear in the background as a kind of low-frequency hum.

When I teach someone to cast (which I absolutely detest doing), I have two modes: the voice where I know the person, and the voice where I don't know the person.

Know The Person Voice

"No, Dumbass. Like this. It's like a metronome. Ten and two. Tick tock. Like the movie. DON'T MOVE YOUR ELBOW LIKE THAT! You're making a whip crack. I don't see the team of horses. Do you see a team of horses? SLOW DOWN."

CRACK.

"For God's sake, DID I TELL YOU NOT TO MOVE YOUR ELBOW LIKE THAT? DON'T MOVE YOUR ELBOW LIKE THAT. What part of don't move your frigging elbow don't you understand?"

Don't Know the Person Voice

"Okay, pretend that the rod is a spaghetti noodle, and it has a certain amount of flex, but if you flex the noodle too much, the noodle will snap. Also recall there is a piece of soft yarn on the end of the spaghetti noodle, and the yarn is the thing being cast, not the fly. Completely different concept. Okay?"

"My noodle broke."

"It's not really a noodle. But if it was, it would be uncooked. It's okay. Pretend it's a buggy whip, but you don't want it to whip. It needs to kind of whip, however, but not that much."

"I'm confused."

"Me, too. Maybe we can just get you a spinning rod with Hello Kitty on the reel."

"Great!"

Of course, I immediately harken back to my early, 15-year-long efforts to learn how to cast. I would stand in my front yard in Arden Hills, Minnesota, and crack the whip. It never seemed to work right. Then I would go down to our forgiving lake down the hill, Lake Johanna, and catch a couple of crappies. I felt like, yeah, I know how to cast. Crappies don't care if you make a crappy cast. However, crappies aren't trout, and trout actually do seem to care about how you make a cast. Lousy cast, no trout. Trout are like the worst, most demanding fly-casting instructors in the world. They let you know without any hesitation whatsoever that you are, in fact, a poor, incompetent, hopelessly inadequate caster. And worse. To add insult to injury, they also don't bother to give you any useful casting tips, which is also usually beyond the skill set of 98 percent of your friends or guides.

Guides, in fact, hate to give casting lessons. I have seen a lot of them do it, and it is not done with relish. Some of them are good casting instructors, in a pinch, because if you don't know what you're doing, then all that happens is you don't catch anything, which is really bad for a guide. No tip, no return trip, no word of mouth. All you would say is "Man, I fished with that guide, and it cost me 300 bucks, plus tip." So any halfway decent guide is going to take the time to get your mind and mend right. I remember going out with one guide on the Williamson River about 15 years ago, and all I had to do in order to catch fish was make a 90-foot cast, placing the very large, wind-resistant *Hexagenia* pattern exactly 3 feet from the nose of the trout, under overhanging brush, into a slight headwind. Child's play, really, except for the fact that making a 90-foot cast is akin to hitting the three-pointer from the concession stand with your eyes closed. Try it. No one makes a 90-foot cast.

Okay, I have seen a few people make 90-foot casts. They were using 10-foot 8-weights, had a tailwind, shooting-head lines, split shot, rocket launchers, and were fingering rosaries the whole time.

So when I was with this guide on the Williamson, we (he) made a few practice casts—"See, it's easy, you just lay it down like that."

Uh-huh.

I felt like some ten-year-old Little League pitcher getting some instruction from Randy Johnson—"See, it's easy, you just throw the ball 99 miles per hour, just like I did."

I closed my eyes, got out the split shot and the rocket launcher and the rosaries, checked the runners at first and third, and made the cast. The fly landed 3 feet up from the trout, 90 feet away, and the trout smashed it. Unfortunately, because there was 90 feet of line out, it took 20 seconds for my hook strike to reach the fly, which was by then drifting innocently downstream and dragging. But I did make the cast. That was my first, and last, 90-foot cast.

I'm not saying casting well is impossible. For example, I have seen some convincing computer animations demonstrating that it can be done, and one time a friend showed me a long mathematical formula illustrating precisely how you can do it. But I think that really getting casting down relies on one thing:

Feel.

How do you explain "feel?"

Hmm. Well. How do you explain chocolate? How do you explain wind? How do you explain God? You can't. You just wake up in the morning, 15 years after you have started fly casting, and there it is. You've figured it out. You know how to fly cast. You can

put it over there, lay it over here, smack it right down yonder, and drop it right in that slot. One day, I just went out and I was able to cast perfectly presented, right-on-the-money, textbook fly casts. By feel. Why? How?

I have no idea.

Once you have taken the 15 years to learn how to fly cast, after your self-esteem has been ground into the dust, after you have destroyed friendships over someone's attempts at casting instruction, after you have felt like a 2-year-old being potty trained, it is then time to learn *different* types of casts.

The first one I was able to really learn was the roll cast. The roll cast is actually pretty easy to do, and it is enormously satisfying. How one would teach someone to execute a roll cast is, again, beyond me, but it can be done, and I do them. I know, I know: Jack, do you know how to tie your shoe? You just kind of, you know, flip the rod tip over ("NO, NOT LIKE THAT—LIKE THIS, DUMBASS!"), and there it is: a roll cast. You can just flip that line over practically right in front of you. It's cool. No, I can't explain it to you.

Once you have mastered the roll cast, you can then move to learning how to double-haul. Now, how anyone can adequately explain double-hauling to anyone is absolutely beyond me. It really is. You have to jerk the line back at some theoretically precise instant as you let go of about 20 or 30 feet of coiled line in your hand, and the line just kind of zips out instantly as you release it from your hand. I have seen illustrations of how to do the double-haul, and, honestly, I think that these pieces of artwork are based on something other than reality like, say, cartoons. Cartoons could adequately convey just how silly double-hauling is. Almost.

Once you've mastered regular missionary casting, the roll cast, and the double-haul, you can move to learning some other casts, like the "S" cast. The "S" cast is pretty self explanatory. You just move your arm—don't ask me to explain it, diagram it, or cartoon it—in a certain way in order to make the line form an "S." Take extra precautions to avoid creating a "Z" cast. These are very tricky. And don't even get me started on the "X" cast. Good luck on that one. I am now working on doing the "@" symbol cast.

There are lots of other casts that fly-fishing writers don't describe, either. There is the dies-in-the-middle cast, which is a fairly common phenomenon. You take the line, making sure that you have slightly less than enough force to adequately propel the line, and somewhere in between about 20 and 40 feet, the line just . . . stops. It hangs in the air for about five seconds, and then falls in a heap right over the rising trout that you are now not going to catch. It actually creates a small splash when it hits the water, alerting all trout in the area that a predator—you (theoretically, anyway)—is in the area. There is also the heavy-plastic-garden-hose cast, which is another abortive attempt to harness physics for peaceful purposes. You use all the techniques of a regular cast, and then all of a sudden it adds 20 pounds in weight and lands in the water like US Airways Flight 1549 dunking in the Hudson. Everyone survives, including the trout. A huge wake emanates outward as the line hits the water, having the practical effect of putting every single trout down like a flock of geese crashing into the riffle.

People often ask me if the rod really makes a difference in your ability to cast, particularly in long-distance casting. I always answer, yes, the rod can make a big difference. If your rod isn't really expensive, you may find it difficult to make any sort of decent, aesthetically pleasing cast at all. And, conversely, I can also tell you that a rod makes almost no difference whatsoever. I saw this guy who worked at a fly shop once make about a 50-foot cast *without even using a rod.*

Then he sold me a Sage rod.

Imagine buying something you have had physically demonstrated that you don't need.

Oh, wait.

That's the cardinal rule of fly fishing.

DESCHUTES

Every angler has a home river. Mine is the Deschutes. I'm not sure the Deschutes will accept me as my home river, and I doubt I am really worthy of having the Deschutes as my home river. I haven't discussed it with whoever is in charge of these things, however, so I have staked it out as my own for now. I probably deserve the Cuyahoga River in Cleveland as my home river, but it hasn't caught fire in a long time, so I am sure it's not as exciting to fish as it was in the 1960s.

The Deschutes is really several different rivers. There's the big canyon huge part of the river, the Lower Deschutes, which is kind of like fishing on Venus, except it's a little cooler on Venus in the summer. This part of the Deschutes has massive canyon walls, is several hundred feet wide, and is loaded with drift boats, rubber rafts, snakes, has railroad tracks running alongside, and is about as much fun to wade as the Amazon when you've got a hemorrhaging cut on your leg. Mostly it's filled with fishermen, many of whom seem to know precisely what they're doing, which, to me, is always a concern: competition. Fly fishermen hate competition.

A lot of people fish the Deschutes for steelhead. I have, and I know it's great and everything, but I just haven't really gotten around to getting serious about steelheading. I should. It would entail having to go get a 14-foot for a 9-weight Spey rod with a shotgun shell on the tip, and I haven't let myself go there yet. I get a lot of invitations to go steelheading by people who are expert at it, but you may have read elsewhere that steelhead are kind of cagey about wanting to be caught. You have to throw these absolutely massive flies around for hours, which means you have to make a billion casts, and usually I just want to actually catch something, even if it's 12 inches. So I don't exploit the steelhead resource that much. One time I hooked a steelhead when I was fly fishing, and it actually scared me it was so big. Of course, it busted off immediately because I was using a 5X leader. I doubt I would have even had a chance with, say, a 6,000-pound chain as tippet material.

The part of the Deschutes that I usually fish is the Middle Deschutes, which is dramatically different than the Lower Deschutes. For example, you are probably not going to die if you fall in, like you would in the Lower Deschutes. If you fall in the Lower Deschutes, I hope you have your papers in order and have left next of kin detailed instructions what to do with your body, which they may or may not find hanging off of a branch. At one launch area, the helpful yet somewhat macabre folks at the Bureau of Land Management (which runs 70 percent of Oregon, and Oregon doesn't seem to realize it or care) have placed on display a mangled aluminum drift boat that looks like a pop can you stepped on for recycling. It's to remind you to wear your life jacket and also recycle.

Taking a float trip down the Deschutes sometimes has the feel of drifting through a *Star Trek* set (and sometimes I've felt like I had about as much chance of catching a trout as I would on a *Star Trek* set), but it is a thrilling experience, particularly as one approaches Whitehorse Rapids. Whitehorse Rapids is a Class 3 chute, and you could see where an inexperienced boat handler might wind up with a crushed pop can (or a pile of really expensive kindling) for a vessel. As you approach the rapids, the guide always starts talking to you like you're on a 737 with one engine out in a thunderstorm. (Attendants tell you to put on your life jackets, assume the position, make real sure you know the location of the exits, and explain the lights on the floor leading to the inflatable slides.) You accelerate quickly, bounce around, and close your eyes a little bit, and then you're through them, and then you're ready not to have any shot at catching fantastic hot redside rainbows in some really good spots.

Fishing the Deschutes is illegal from a boat, so most of the action is either walking on the bank or wading very carefully so that you don't step out into *The Abyss*, which was a movie starring Ed Harris about fishing the Deschutes. The drop-offs are similar to those one would encounter if the Grand Canyon were completely filled with water and there had been a heavy rainstorm the night before. There would be a fairly good advantage to fishing the Deschutes if you were an orangutan, because mostly the drill is swinging from branch to branch, making almost impossibly difficult sidearm casts. This presupposes that orangutans can cast; I certainly can see where the typical orangutan is a better caster than I am.

The part I enjoy fishing the most is the Middle Deschutes, and I am going to go into very little detail here. Fly-fishing writers always blow their spots, and I am always very—um—not forthcoming about my spots and their specific charms. For example, if you chloroformed me, blindfolded me, drove me 300 miles out of town, put me in the Federal Witness Protection Program, and had three

CIA case officers work me over in a jail cell with a single lightbulb, I may crack enough to tell you that the Middle Deschutes is in Oregon, it has trout in it, and I am familiar with some of the patterns necessary to catch fish. That would be about as far as I would go with my interrogation. Unless, of course, you gave me a piece of pie. Then I would probably crack and tell you that the Middle Deschutes was composed entirely of two parts hydrogen and one part oxygen. But it would have to be really good pie.

The stretch that I have fished has a mix of browns and rainbows in it. I wouldn't say they are incredibly difficult to catch. It's more like any river, which would be that if you happen to know what's coming off on the hatch and you have that pattern, and if you can get to the rising fish, and you can make the cast, then you're probably going to catch a fish or two. Or not. I like this part of the river because it's pretty manageable and attractive; I also like the fact that the snake factor is pretty low. On the Lower Deschutes, it is not at all unusual to make acquaintance with rattlesnakes. Historically, I have not liked rattlesnakes, and in the Lower Deschutes, they're in the road, hiding in rocks, lying under brush, and generally trying to figure out ways to bite you. I have been eternally vigilant about hand placement on the Lower Deschutes as I have climbed up and down the basalt rock walls.

There are several flies that I would not be without on the Deschutes, and they make no sense whatsoever. For the dry flies, one is the Royal Wulff, which imitates nothing but a bad acid trip, and a Yellow Humpy, which imitates absolutely nothing in the insect world, but kind of resembles a 1959 Studebaker if it were made out of deer hair. I would also take along a cased-caddis pattern, which is probably, next to the San Juan Worm, the easiest fly to tie in the world. I would bring along a few different caddis patterns as well, and a black Bunny Leech the size of a rattlesnake. Just in case.

The big event of the year on the Deschutes is the Salmonfly hatch, and a Kaufmann's Stimulator or a Clark's Stone works great. As I walk in downtown Portland in early June, I can actually hear people discussing the Salmonfly hatch on the street. Non-fishing legal secretaries at Starbucks getting a triple Americano talk about the Salmonfly hatch. It's like a low murmur in the air: "Blah blah blah they're really heavy out this year blah blah blah he caught 16 the other day in a half hour blah blah blah smashed it under a tree blah blah blah." Usually when I get around to it, I will either be a shade early or a touch late on hitting the hatch, but it's really exciting fishing and pretty easy. It's like floating PowerBait.

The Upper Deschutes is quite narrow, has brookies and rainbows, and is definitely a small-rod experience, unlike the Lower Deschutes. The Upper Deschutes originates in the Cascade Lakes Highway area above Bend, and it's gorgeous, particularly around Little Lava Lake. I don't think you can fish that part now, but I did 25 years ago when I first moved out here, and it was pretty forgiving. There are other attractions around there—Wickiup and Crane Prairie Reservoirs among them, as well as a lake that's stocked with Atlantic salmon. I tried it once when I didn't know what I was doing, along with my brother-in-law, who didn't know what he was doing, either. Two people fly fishing who do not know what they're doing is usually a fatal combination; they tend to ratify each other's mistakes and worst instincts, like a drunk pilot and co-pilot.

"I think that's Cleveland up ahead. Bob, does that look like Cleveland?"

"Roger, Cleveland or Cincinnati, one of the two. Let's put her down and see what happens."

"Columbus, maybe."

"It's Ohio. Close enough."

I have fished on the Deschutes for 25 years or so, and I still feel like I am playing defense the whole time. If you hit it right, well, it is one of the greatest rivers in the world, you're a genius, and one of America's Next Hot Fly Fishermen. If you blow it, it's just almost surreal in its ability to humble you; trout will be rising everywhere, and you're just a man trying not to fall in the water. Some days, I have walked miles and miles along the Deschutes under ideal conditions and have never even seen credible evidence that it was a trout river, and the next time it's like fishing at Uncle Frank's Trout-O-Rama Kiddie Pond.

One of the most intriguing experiences I have had on the Deschutes was being invited to fish on the Deschutes Club, which is a private stretch on the Lower Deschutes managed by a small group of landowners who literally inherited the right to fish it from their fathers and grandfathers. There is a 50-year waiting list. I am not joking. People have lived full, rich lives and died of natural causes at age 99 waiting to get into the Deschutes Club. The club was started in the 1930s by a group of Portland businessmen and political types, who, rightly or wrongly, bought up a bunch of ranches and locked the gate. There have been bills introduced into the Oregon legislature to unlock the gate. There have been lawsuits filed as regularly as a caddis hatch to unlock the gate. They have never been successful. You are permitted to walk in, but that is a long walk and the sun burns at two million degrees Fahrenheit in the summer. Rafters and guides can stop at a few designated camps along the club, but otherwise you can just forget it. I was invited to fish it a few times, and finally went not long ago. Before I was invited, I was of the opinion that it was not a good idea to lock the gate. Having fished it, I am now of the opinion that it's a good idea because it gives the trout a long stretch where they really can thrive, and it's helpful to the rest of the river up- and downstream. Of course, it fished very well, but I have certainly had similar success on other parts of the river around there. It's very well managed. I will continue to have that opinion even if I never get invited back. Based on my casting ability, that is always a possibility.

One of the odder aspects of the Deschutes is that it seems to fish counterintuitively to most other Western rivers. Since you can't fish it out of a boat, I can tell you after drifting it many times that there are very few big gravel bars that you can just wade out and have your Big Western River on a Magazine Cover Experience. It is an incredibly slippery bottom—my friend says it's like walking on slimy bowling balls. I thought it was more like a river designed by Neil Armstrong: a small step followed by a giant leap into the drink.

I feel extraordinarily fortunate to have the Deschutes in my life. It's kind of like having your best friend from high school happen to live in the same place you do, and you can go back and relive years of good memories without self-consciousness or fear of making a mistake.

"Hey, remember that time you stood for three hours in the same spot and threw the same Floatin' Fool over and over, dragging all over the place, and it was 94 degrees, and I finally let you catch one because I felt sorry for you?"

"Dude, thanks. You're a pal."

Like a real friend, the Deschutes knows all of your foibles, faults, and failures, and ultimately forgives.

THE DAY I DIED WHILE FLY FISHING

K elly Creek, Idaho, is not where I thought I would die. I guess we all run these theoretical how-it's-gonna-happen-and-where scenarios, but the thing is, you probably don't know when you've died, anyway, so what's the point? I know that I had frequently envisioned worst-case death scenarios: falling through the ice, burning under a tanker in a car crash, victim of a holdup, or worse, but I am able to quickly put them out of my mind, like all those bad thoughts I have about why I can't get my heavily Gehrke's Ginked fly to float. I have to say, however, that dying while fly fishing is simply a model I haven't studied. Not that we get a choice. Well, sometimes you do, but even then, it's probably a bad decision. People always say that you have to live with your decisions, but if you kill yourself, well, you don't have to live with that one. I have only wanted to kill myself while breaking off fly after fly on backcasts during a good hatch. The rest of the time, I'm fine.

And when I was in my late 20s, I was really fine: nice family, nice house, nice car, good health—except for my death in Kelly Creek, Idaho. If you do have to die, Kelly Creek is probably a really good place to do so: pretty good cutthroat fishing, beautiful scenery, clear water, the occasional elk splashing across the river, and no telephones—except at the local Kelly Forks Ranger Station, where they have a radiophone. I had only been involved in one other near-death experience on a fly-fishing trip, and that was with a friend who fell off a big rock. I was standing right behind him, and he just tripped and disappeared off the cliff, like Wile E. Coyote. The poor guy landed almost headfirst about 10 feet from the edge of the rock, broke his collarbone (and his rod), and we had to send him to a hospital that was about 70 miles downriver from Nowhere. There were two ambulance changes. It was that remote. We thought he might have broken his neck or something worse, but he was discharged from the hospital that night, arm in a sling. He fished with his arm in a sling for the next three days. That is really hard to do—try it sometime. He caught a lot of fish, too. But my death was even more dramatic than that.

The thing that interests me about dying is the whole What Do You Do While You're Dead question. Is death boring? Is it psychedelic? Is it foggy? It's hard to imagine it as nothingness; if it is, then, well, there are a lot of things like death/nothingness in real life: Walmart parking lots, for example. I suppose we all have our private heaven or hell in mind, depending on our religious teachings or lack thereof. I have to say, I was *really* happy with my afterlife at Kelly Creek. It was everything any true fly fisherman could have hoped for. I was traipsing along the banks of a stunning Idaho creek, catching fairly good cutts and rainbows in most of the pools, or at least getting interesting takes. I was fishing with a large, easily visible Royal Wulff pattern that I am quite certain I never broke off during my afterlife. I had some food with me. I had a water bottle. The weather was great, but I was able to fish in shade, making it even more pleasant. In short, Death was Good.

I am not quite sure how I died on Kelly Creek, either. I may have slipped and hit my head on a rock, or I could have had some weird fainting spell and fallen into the river and drowned. With me, the clumsiness-as-cause-of-death possibilities are endless.

Since I can report that there is an afterlife, I can also report what goes through your mind when you're dead. Mostly, it's the same stuff we have while living, except it seems a little farther away. I do specifically recall an afterlife thought about how I needed another PowerBar. I am not sure why we have to eat in the afterlife, but we do. Oh, some of the other thoughts I had:

1. This fly keeps dragging.

2. The tippet is too big.

3. Maybe I should change flies.

Remarkably, I had virtually the same thoughts and frustrations in death that I had in life—it reminded me of this movie I just saw about people who had committed suicide. In their afterlife, the world was tackier and even less aesthetically pleasing than their real, previous life. If a fly fisherman had committed suicide in this movie, he would have wound up fishing with a Sears automatic reel from the 1950s and a rod that had duct tape all over it. That is not my idea of hell, but it would be some sort of purgatory.

So I was happily enjoying the afterlife on Kelly Creek, even though I was not, in fact, aware that I was a) dead and b) in the hereafter. I had been fishing for about five hours in the Kelly Creek Postlife Environment. I had left my party, which consisted of my friends Jim Ramsey, Dick Thomas, and my dad. Now, my dad and I have had many misadventures while fishing for trout. In fact, it was kind of a given that anytime we actually went fishing, something weird, bad, or comically unexpected happened. It became a kind of joke: his 24-inch rainbow that had broken off on the propeller of

the engine (all he did when I was a kid was yell at me about keeping the line away from the propeller), the time I tried to get a huge
northern in the boat when I was 12 (he kept saying, trancelike, as
he was reeling it in: "This is the biggest fish I have ever hooked
in my life") and knocked the hook out of its mouth with the too-
small net, and about 34 other things. One time we were in a boat
that was sinking but managed to make it to shore during a gale in
a reservoir in Utah—that was the worst. But I didn't die on any of
those trips. Until this trip.

At around eight o'clock, as the light was fading, I had just
caught a nice 12-inch rainbow—one of the few I had seen on Kelly
Creek. I walked back up the bank to the gravel road to catch up
to everyone. It had occurred to me that I hadn't seen any of them
in a long time. I was wondering what had happened to them, but
no matter, this sort of thing happened all the time. Sometimes you
walked a mile or two, and there they all were, you hooked up,
exchanged the damage report, and went back to the car or the
truck. End of story.

This time, as I walked along the road, I sensed something was
wrong. I hadn't seen them all in hours, and it was getting to be
pulling-up-stakes time, and we needed to drive all the way back to
this cabin we were staying at on the Lochsa, I think it was. It was
at least a two-hour drive, and I was out of PowerBars. I walked for
a few minutes, and then all sorts of thoughts flashed through my
head: *Did their car go off into the river? Did they take off without
me? Were they mad? How many had they caught?* How many had
they caught was the predominant thought, as it would be with any
serious fly fisherman. You could be with a party, they could have all
been abducted by Martians or Romulans, or perhaps been held hos-
tage for a day by Al Qaeda, and when you saw them, the first thing
that you would probably say to them was, "Did you get any?" They

could be bleeding, decapitated, or burned beyond recognition, and you would still ask that. That's how fly fishermen are.

The light was now very low. In the distance on the road I could make out three figures slowly approaching me in the twilight. The quality of the light was kind of golden—the kind of light that you would see in a movie about a near-death experience where your grandparents and Uncle Bob and your kindergarten teacher from 1965 would all be drifting toward you in that brilliant light—and it was really kind of beautiful. As they came into focus, their facial expressions were those of someone who had just been told that there was a Mr. Rod Serling here to see them, and that there was a signpost up ahead, and the next stop was *The Twilight Zone*.

They just stood there, and very rarely do you see people with their mouths all simultaneously agape. Finally, I said what was on my mind, and what would be on the mind of any self-respecting fly fisherman:

"I really hammered them! I caught a really great rainbow down there around the bend, and I must have caught 20 nice fish. Did you guys get anything?"

I am sure I was smiling. They weren't. No response.

I said, gamely, "What's the matter?"

My dad said, "I'm just glad to see you, son." His face was streaked with tears.

"What the hell is the matter. Didn't you catch anything?" I am known for my sensitive and thoughtful deflecting when I see faces streaked with tears. Minnesota people always want to change the subject when they see tear-streaked faces.

My friend Jim's face wasn't tear-streaked. His face turned angry.

"We thought you were dead, you son of a bitch."

"Um. No. I am not dead. Why did you think I was dead?"

"You weren't supposed to get ahead of us."

"Yeah, but the fishing was so good that I . . ."

"You weren't supposed to get ahead of us. We've been looking for you for hours. We thought you were dead." Sensing that I was about to become dead, again, I went into my speed-apology rap, which any married person knows full well how to execute in key situations. That didn't help.

My dad then said, "I was trying to find your father-in-law's phone number so we could call him and have him tell your wife that you were missing and maybe dead. We thought you had drowned."

Um. Oh boy.

So I offered to buy dinner. On me! At the chicken place!

"You bastard. You're goddamned right you're buying."

Dick seemed particularly upset, although I thought the news that I had offered to buy dinner, a rare occurrence, would cheer him.

"Get in the %$@*!!! car."

Twenty years later, they are still kind of grumpy about it.

I hate death.

WHO IS A FLY FISHERMAN?

A friend of mine who sensibly has thus far not taken up fly fishing posed the question, "Just what kind of person fly fishes, anyway?"

I have spent weeks pondering this.

For starters, fly fishermen—the good ones—have what I would call a certain attention to detail, a hyperawareness of the most minute changes in the environment, and are goal-oriented people. Some people would call them obsessive, which is true. Obsessive people prefer to be told that they have attention to detail. This is all parsing, really, but when you get a bunch of people together who can have an animated discussion about precisely what angle would be ideal to set a Microfibett tail on a mayfly imitation, you also have a bunch of people who notice things in other aspects of their lives.

Excuse me for a moment. I have to go check the locks and make sure the gas is turned off and wash my hands and make my forks all go the right direction in the silverware drawer.

No, wait. It's okay.

I would say there are the experts, who can border on really hideous tedium (*hideum?*) with their Latin, fluorocarbon, and *cul de canard* hot gas. There are very good fly fishermen, who know what they're doing, cast well, and catch fish routinely.

Just because I have written a number of silly books about fly fishing doesn't mean that I am an expert fly fisherman: I am not, not by a long shot. I know nothing about

1. Bonefishing. Next to nothing. I mean, flats, sighting, long casts, bad sunburns—that's it.

2. I couldn't begin to tell you how to use a whip finisher. No clue. None.

3. Spey rods—zip.

4. How to really catch a steelhead. I know I should know this. I live in Oregon, for God's sake. I mean, I could go out and try to catch one, ask around the fly shop for some good patterns, and wing it, but, honestly, I don't know jack about it.

5. Many of the articles in the fly magazines I kind of skip through, particularly the ones about insects or streamflows.

6. I am not sure exactly what to call that little shiny knob on the fly reel that has nothing to do with anything I can figure out.

7. I am a little unsure about how to tie some obvious fly patterns.

8. If awakened in the middle of the night, I probably would not be able to tell the difference between a Cream Cahill and a Light Hendrickson.

9. If I were taking water temperature, and I knew what it was, I am not sure I could do anything about it.

Still, I would say I am a good fly fisherman, which is about as far as I am willing to pat myself on the back. I would say that most of my friends also fall in that category. They go out 10 or 15 times a year, they talk about it a lot, they own some nice gear, and they spend some time thinking about it. But mostly, they work as accountants, writers, copy editors, physicians, bankers, lawyers, stockbrokers, contractors, and in other trades that require that T's are crossed and I's are dotted.

Then there is the third category: Anglers Who Do Not Know What in God's Green Earth They Are Doing. I see them all the time. They stand in the wrong spot, precisely blocking you from getting into the right spot. They use odd, antiquated fly patterns and brag about it. They have reels I have never heard of. They drink beer while they fish, not after. I am not a prude or Cary Nation, but for some reason it just drives me crazy when fly fishermen drink while they fish. In bass fishing, it is practically a given that you have to be a little faced in order to have fun; it's part of the deal, along with operating a large watercraft unsafely and at high speed. Drinking after is, of course, fine, expected, and helps you calm down from a long day of absolute failure.

Fly fishing with doctors is something I generally haven't done; but the ones I have fished with, well, let's just say they're good with knots. Asking a doctor in Oregon if he's a fly fisherman is almost oxymoronic; it's like asking him if he golfs or has $56K in checking. I haven't met one yet who wasn't a fly fisherman, and they're ALL good. If he isn't a good fly fisherman, well, let's just say I would get a second opinion. You don't want a doctor who isn't dexterous with small, sharp objects. I also feel safer fishing when I'm with a doctor; I like the certain knowledge that he can repair my compound-complex leg fracture I got from slipping down the bank. Of course, he would probably break my rod and lash it to my leg as a splint, and then I wouldn't want to fish with him anymore.

I have also fished with some lawyers. Lawyers are not as legalistic in person as they are in their jobs—many of them, in fact, seem somewhat devil-may-care, particularly on the trout stream. I suspect it's because they have all those rules they have to observe in real life. I know one woman who became a lawyer simply because she enjoyed writing nasty letters. There are no nasty letters in fly fishing. There are regulations in fly fishing, but I never hear the lawyers talk about them. I think what lawyers and doctors have in common, at least on the stream, is the observance of some sort of order. Good doctors and lawyers are, ideally, orderly: they make the proper prescriptions and diagnoses, and follow the correct legal forms and protocol. Fly fishing has something of the same kind of order, with the same potential for a potentially unpleasant outcome. You choose the right fly, the right tippet diameter, make the right presentation, and put the fly in the right spot, and maybe it all works out.

Then again, maybe it doesn't.

Lawyers and doctors I have known who have fly fished have been very gear-oriented. Same thing with CEOs or people who owned small businesses whom I have fished with; they are used to high-quality equipment and instruments in their professions, and this translates over into their hobby. I also see this with camera people. Don't get me started on camera people, but an unusually high percentage of fly-fishing nuts are also shutterbugs. Ideally, fly-fishing nuts should be called fly-fishing bugs. At least the idiom matches up.

People who are in, shall we say, more gestural professions seem to be less rigorous about what kind of gear they have. Sales guys

almost never talk about their stuff, in my experience. They are more interested in the numbers. I am fairly distrustful of anglers who give me an exact count of how many they caught, how many they lost, and how many takes they had. Plus, they're lying most of the time, anyway. Interestingly, my accountant fishing buddy is pretty much all Oh-I-Lost-Count-ish about his numbers. I hardly ever want to hear that my accountant lost count of something, but I think it shows his essentially good-natured attitude toward the whole enterprise.

As in golf, there are hackers and people with low handicaps in fly fishing. The low-handicap crowd tends to take it all a little too seriously, but they are enormously helpful to regular slobs like me who are always asking obvious questions. These types are useful to have around because they can always be counted upon to have the ability to bang out a good nail knot, or give you a solid read on whether the *Callibaetis* is mottled or not. They even sometimes seem to actually enjoy helping. A good streamside coach can either be incredibly annoying or marvelously useful, depending on his tone of voice—like a wife.

More often that not, fly fishermen can't really be broken down into a reliable stereotype. For example, as a political cartoonist, I trend very much toward a more *laissez-faire* attitude about it all, and I do like to ghillie for someone and simply watch and coach, even if it's simple directions like "Keep moving" or "There's a nice rise over there—cover that." Sometimes I drift into outright pedantry, which is accepted by fly anglers, because they enjoy that sort of thing.

Probably one of the truly great fly fishermen I have ever known was my Uncle Hal Jensen, even as he seemed to prefer using monstrous Helin Frog Flatfish to troll, or tiny Triple Teazers. Hal was very much in the category of, hey, whatever works, Ace . . . you wanna catch fish or not? No one was really quite certain what Hal did for a living. He "retired" at 49 from Commercial Credit in Utah, and spent the next 30 years hanging around his ratty trailer up on Strawberry Reservoir near Salt Lake City. Strawberry was at the time a marvelously reliable fishery, and if Hal told us we were gonna get up at 4:30 AM and troll so we could catch some big rainbows or cutts, we got up at 4:30 AM and trolled, and there would be big rainbows and cutts, as promised. I mean, you could see all the stars and there wasn't light for another hour—pitch black. He used ocean trolling rods because his arms wouldn't get tired, and sometimes the fish were so big that those rods were a great idea.

If he said to tie on one of his comically long-shanked Renegades, that's how it was going down. You did it. Uncle Hal had been in the Army engineers at D-Day—he landed at Utah Beach, ironically—and stood in the water for six hours. Because there was so much traffic on the beach as the LSTs stacked up in a monumental jam, he physically couldn't get ashore. He just stood there in the water carrying his full pack and rifle and waited. Once he did land, he was one of the many engineers who helped build the first dock at Normandy, which enabled all the ships to tie up and dump supplies. I doubt he even got a medal any higher that a combat infantry badge, but he was just one of the two million people in World War II who quietly did his job and won the war without advertising it. Not a hero in the way we now think about it, but I think his war experience helped him apply a rather workmanlike approach to fly fishing: get out there, get the job done, come back in one piece.

I guess we should call his school of thought Realpolitik Trout Fishing, not fly fishing, really, because he was so methodical about his methodology. Flies, flatfish, worms, whatever. Velveeta was a bait of choice on a cheese hook—it works like a charm—and one of his favorite tactics was to chum with cheap corn. The corn would drift slowly into the olive water, and occasionally a trout would come up in the weeds and snatch it away before we could troll through the flak curtain. A three-pound cutt or a rainbow that ran 20 inches was an unremarkable fish for him, and he only seemed to get excited if the trout was over five pounds.

One night, Hal noticed some swirling fish just offshore from his trailer. He threw on some gaudy fly of his own concoction—they were large and beautifully tied, but God knows what actual pattern, if any, they were—and he caught five brook trout in one small spot that ran about two pounds or so per fish, and were colored like a Utah sunset: bright reds, optic oranges, and deep yellows with indigo splashes.

Hal was not above employing even more nefarious tactics than flatfish, but he held anglers who used cowbells—he called them "Ford Fenders"—in complete contempt. "Hell's Bells," he would mutter, "you can't even tell if you got a goddamned fish on it or not." He was kind of like the Malcolm X of trout, a by-any-means-necessary kind of fisherman, but he preferred to throw a fly with a bubble around at twilight if they were rising. That was his idea of fly fishing, using a bubble. I don't think I ever saw him use a fly rod. We would catch a bunch of huge trout, get done by 9 AM or so, then go back and eat a big pile of greasy eggs and bacon. Maybe he would have a Jim Boomer as an aperitif.

One time, a gale blew up on the Strawberry. I knew we were in trouble because I would huddle under the bow of the boat if it was too splashy, and Hal and my dad told me to get out and get my life jacket on. I was instructed to start bailing as six-foot waves crashed over the bow. We must have been out in the reservoir for over an hour as the storm pelted us with stinging rain and the boat was full of large hail pellets. By the time we got back to the dock, which we executed a two-point carrier landing on because of the waves—BANG!—then another wave and then BANG! . . . we jumped out and half-swam back to the trailer through the undulating water. When we got back to the trailer, my dad asked me if I wanted a drink.

I was ten, so I passed and had a Shasta Orange, my beverage of choice. It wasn't Scotch, but hey, it seemed to work. Maybe dad spiked it.

Several years later, my dad, who had survived multiple close calls in the Korean War (one time, he was running down a hill, and the soldier in front of him had his head completely shot off onto my dad's chest, and the soldier behind him was also killed, and my dad hid behind a rock for six hours, then ran three miles back to his unit—he got no medal for that, either), told me that he was utterly convinced we were going to drown in the icy waters of Strawberry Reservoir. My dad is not prone to exaggerate—if anything, he underplays—and I felt that electric jolt of existential fear that all people who brush close to death feel, but my jolt was years later after the fact.

In my experience with all the different types of fly fishermen, the ones I respond to the most are the ones like Uncle Hal. He just liked catching the fish, and he wasn't a snob about how he got there.

And he did draw the line at Ford Fenders.

Me, too.

They are really hard to use with a 5-weight.

BOOK REVIEW

Reflections on My Fly: Fly-Tying Tricks 'n' Tips, and Other
Philosophical Musings on the Meaning of Angling Life.

By Jack Ohman, Adipose Press Publishing Group, 762 pages.
Reviewed by Michiko Kakutani.

Mr. Ohman, a newspaper artist and writer toiling away in Oregon drawing silly pictures of the president's ears, has created what has to be the most lugubrious pile of drivel in the history of American fly-angling literature. No, the reader is not kidding. It will make you want to switch to worm-and-bobber fishing.

Mr. Ohman fills this massive turgid screed with almost laughable literary allusions, inept metaphors, sentences that meander around the manuscript like tributaries of some polluted river, and disturbingly maudlin non sequiturs that leave the reader not only not wanting more, but leading anyone sentient to have the overwhelming sensation of wanting to drown Mr. Ohman in any given available body of good trout water.

Mr. Ohman, who spent over six years crafting what reads like an 11th-grade creative writing project finished at 5:15 the morning it was due, commences writing the Great American Fly Fishing Novel, abruptly changes the book to a how-to book about fly tying, switches over to a series of essays, and then morphs into a rambling diatribe. Mr. Melville, meet Mr. Schwiebert and Mr. Kaczynski.

Mr. Ohman's first stab at some sort of a plotline concerns an armless fly fisherman named Ahab and his pursuit of a Great White Trout, which strains taxonomic credulity. Mr. Ohman offers no explanation about how an armless angler would even be capable of such a pursuit, but this does not deter Mr. Ohman in the least bit from trying this gambit; he is only able to sustain the novel part of the book for about 20 pages. Then he changes the trout to a carp, thinking the reader will get the joke. He throws in a barbless harpoon and a narrator named "Izzy."

The fly-tying part of the book is 230 pages of factual errors, poorly described techniques, and ineffective strategies. For example, Mr. Ohman advises the reader to "use dryer lint and dog fur mixed together" in order to achieve the most natural body effect for tying nymphs. The text is riddled with inaccuracy: "my favorite hooks are Mustard [sic]," he notes. The reader is bombarded with ridiculous hints, such as "I collect all hair from the bathtub drain and wrap it up around a streamer hook" and "I have used all the different feathers from a dead robin to make a perfect emerger." The book reads like a transcript from a cross between a mental hospital intake session and an Orvis fly-fishing school. At the end of this part of the book, Mr. Ohman concludes that he "really doesn't know anything about this subject at all, but I know that how-to books sell better."

When Mr. Ohman moves to the essay format in this disjointed car wreck of a volume, he somehow manages to offer a glimpse into what is a mind the size of a trout brain: a tiny, reactive piece of goo that is only capable of survival, not coherent thought. In the essay intriguingly entitled "Metamorphosis Redux," Mr. Ohman puts himself in the place of an emerging mayfly on his back, struggling to rise to the surface "against the strong current that is life itself." In "The Old Man and the Seam," the author tries to chronicle the epic struggle between man and fish as a meta-theme, describing an elderly gentleman in his late 40s attempting to tie on a fly, without reading glasses or the now-bygone ability to hop from boulder to boulder. This passage is barely in English, let alone publishable:

"As I watched the beautiful iridescent rainbow trout hop contentedly out of the water from whence man originated from the primordial soup, his desire to take oxygen and move from the surly bonds of river and touch the face of my size 12 Flashabou Humpy ever obvious and indeed completely a metaphor for living itself, a contest between the known and the unknowable, between the safety of the flowing current and the madness that is modernity, I was reminded once again how much in commonality terms my brother trout and I shared: the desire to be free, to be real, yo, and to eat something fat and juicy."

Agh.

There's more. Trout become "shiny slimy spotted denizens of the wine-dark pool." Flies are described as "tasty fuzzy faux morsels." Fly rods are "dowsing switches to match man against fish." Floatant is "a chemical gooplike amalgam to offer buoyancy in a chaotic wet wilderness." Hooks are "pointy sentinels, ever honed to ensnare and capture barblessly the squirming

foe." Rivers become "capillaries of troutality, the ever-flowing circulatory system of trout's habitat, of which the fish is but a platelet and man is the caring physician." Fellow anglers are "comrades in arms, if we were actually armed." And so on.

This section dribbles on and on, limning the depths of hyperbolic sentence construction. Finally, Mr. Ohman concludes with what appears to be a fly-fishing manifesto of sorts, 256 pages of unpunctuated nonsensical ramblings about "The fly fishing Man" and his efforts to destroy the world with unbridled corporate greed and overpriced tackle—it's like *On the Road* for fly fishermen if the writer was locked in a hypnotic trance. To wit:

" . . . I was standing in the stream and looking and fishing and feeling and wishin' and hopin' and prayin' that America would listen to my pleas (LISTEN AMERICA FOR ONCE) for a just and humane world where the Fascist Fly-Fishing Power Structure would be overthrown by the little fly fisherman and there would be no more SUVs with vanity plates at the trailhead that said KATCH1 and FLYBOY and NOBARB and PMDAOK and that their GORE-

TEXAN Peerless Leonard Hardy Wheatley Old Europe weltanschauung zeitgeist would give way to a new revolutionary paradigm where everyone would be able to fish on Halliburton's private spring creeks and the CIA and the NSA and the FBI would come clean and release their files on me . . . "

Perhaps the most disturbing part of the book is not the book itself, but the endnotes and the index. For example, under the letter "C" we find:

"Caddises, and the way they can sometimes fly into your ears and you squash them and how gross it is, p. 167."

An endnote section reveals a long and troubling paean to a girlfriend from 1977, which has nothing to do whatsoever with fly fishing, and makes reference to "the time when we went to *Saturday Night Fever* and I thought it was really a stupid movie, and how I kept saying that all through the movie, and you finally poured a Coke over my head and walked out of the theater. Then, when I saw the movie again on cable the other night, it seemed pretty good."

You get the picture. Throw in the drawings Mr. Ohman executed for the book, which he apparently drew with a red crayon on a cocktail napkin, and you have a book that is to writing as William Hung is to pop music.